LOVE IN A TIME OF EXTINCTION

Navigating an Eco-Apocalypse

Anne Geraghty

Copyright © Anne Geraghty

The right of Anne Geraghty to be identified as the author of this work has been asserted in accordance with the copyright, designs and Patents Act 1988

Published 2022

Back cover picture:
An ark built by David Blair and Tighnabruaich's Extinction Rebellion.

This is not a book like a biography or a detective story, to read with your feet up and a glass of wine. It is more one to dip into when you feel like it – though you might need the wine. It is an invitation to explore hidden dynamics more than a book with answers.

The book has four themes. One examines what is actually happening to the ecosystems of life on our planet. Another looks at how we have got ourselves to this eco-crisis and why we are not managing to deal with it. Another theme explores what freedom, compassion, integrity and love might look like when life as we know it ceases. The fourth looks at how we might navigate a future that will be challenging us on every level.

I hope there'll be parts that reach you just as I'm sure there'll be parts that do not speak to you at all. There are several chapters about death for example and these may not be anything you need or are remotely interested in – that is apart from preparing for the vast deaths of the 6th Mass Extinction. If all else fails, just read the cartoons.

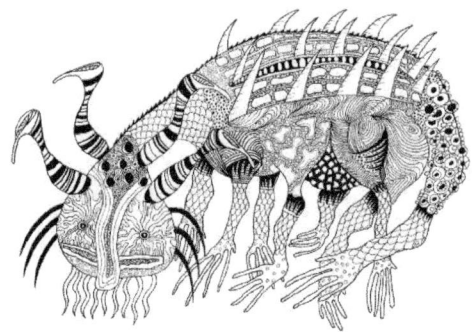

If what's going on gets too much, you've always got denial.

DOWN TO EARTH AND UP TO US

I was born in England into a world rebuilding itself after WW2. Humanity had been horrified by the hell we had created in the form of concentration camps, atomic bombs, firestorms, fascism, mass starvation, mass murder, medical experiments, torture, and scenes of horror on a scale beyond anything seen before. The shock led to the creation of the U.N., the first National Health Service, free education for all and an era of expansion and hope. My mother's family had been poor Irish who could not afford medical care or schooling beyond the age of 14. Out of seven children in her family four died before the age of five from malnutrition and pneumonia, the diseases of poverty. Although my family was poor, I was given free schooling, free health care, free school meals and free university education. I was one of the first working class people to be given such freedom anywhere in the world. And I ran with it. Though I had to run partly to reach escape velocity from a childhood dominated by the Catholic Church.

I loved the world. It was full of amazing things and adventures beyond anything my ancestors had experienced or dreamed of. No one from my family had ever travelled except as cannon fodder in wars. I travelled for fun and adventure, to meet people from different cultures, to see the wonders of the world. You did not need to be rich for this. You simply worked for a while, saved some money, took off and had adventures.

There was of course evil in the shadows. Nuclear weapons, the US war in Vietnam, apartheid in South Africa, the tanks rolling into Dubcek's Czechoslovakia, the lobotomised patients in the locked back wards of mental hospitals, the restricted lives of working class people who had not had my luck and gone to university. The more I began to enjoy the freedoms and adventures of my life, the more I saw how impoverished so many other people's lives were. It felt wrong.

I studied psychology at university. I learned a lot about rats in mazes, how memory works and the physiology of the brain, but not as much as I had hoped about myself, what made so many people unhappy and why we cause so much harm to each other, animals and life. I began to look for other ways to live without the alienation from our natural selves and the chronic unhappiness I saw in so many people.

A group of us set up a commune where we hoped to find new ways to alleviate poverty, injustice and misery. We danced to new music. We explored ourselves and each other in encounter groups. We took LSD to expand our consciousness. We sat through interminable meetings, interminable because everyone had to agree on everything, even everyday decisions like what kind of tea to buy. In another commune we tried to break down 'bourgeois individualistic conditioning' by owning nothing personally. Clothes, shoes, even toothbrushes and beds, were up for grabs on a daily basis. I learned a lot more about people this way than I ever did in my psychology degree or Ph.D. Many bitter fights and commune splits later I realised I needed to dive deeper into the mysteries of the human heart and the politics of experience.

I went to the Dialectics of Liberation conference in 1967 where, among others, I met R.D. Laing, Allen Ginsberg and Stokely Carmichael - each an education beyond any academic course at a university. I became involved in the anti-psychiatry movement trying to find the meaning of mental health issues in terms of the power politics of society, the alienation of modern culture from our natural selves and the chronic unhappiness of a society in which love and freedom were pushed aside in the pursuit of profit and power. I explored our potential for love, consciousness and freedom in encounter groups and primal therapy, trying to move beyond the rigidities and restrictions of a class-ridden society. And when the Women's Liberation Movement erupted I raised my consciousness about feminism and how we had banished the goddess to wilderness. Yet no matter how sincere our good intentions to free humanity from its chains, in order everyone also could have endless meetings and more parties, the world resisted our attempts to change it. I also discovered the seeds of unhappiness lay not only in the politics and injustices of society; they lay within each of us.

When encounter groups, primal therapy, re-birthing and bioenergetics did not shift the struggles in our various communes, I decided more radical change was needed. I travelled to India to learn from the wisdom of the east. Many transformational journeys later I returned to London and ran a centre for therapy and meditation. Twenty years ago however I realised the times of seeking personal freedom and enlightenment were over; there was something far more important than the personal politics of human liberation for its own sake demanding our attention – the future of life on Earth.

Life on this planet is in dire straits. We must deal with the challenges of climate chaos, environmental catastrophe and mass extinction or die. Yet nothing significant on the scale needed is being done. It has become apparent that the global industrial-military complex, international corporate greed, the mass consumerism of modern capitalism, the energy companies with their trillions of dollars profit, the ruthless hunting and killing of animals, the destruction and pollution of forests, rivers, land and sea, together with our human addiction to power over life, material forms of happiness, and alienation for our own animal nature, are not changing.

We can demonstrate, sign petitions, recycle, glue ourselves to the roads, infiltrate and kick up a scene at Davos all we like - but it has become clear this does not shift the entrenched vested interests of the behemoths of power and their destructive exploitation of life. As a consequence, the challenge is no longer how to avert this catastrophe; it has become how to navigate it. We can no longer hope that the corporate world will wake up, politicians will be galvanised into action or that science will save us in some techno-utopian fantasy. We have to deal with this ourselves.

Through all my adventures I learned that when people get together with a common purpose to work for justice, freedom, love, truth, consciousness or however we describe the goodness of life we are seeking, something important always emerges. It may not be what we wanted or hoped for but it is always creative, enlightening, profound and soulful. It is as if an energy field is created, a group soul or team spirit, that itself becomes a source of intelligent guidance. I am suggesting that the creation of this kind of energy field might be one way through the global eco-catastrophe. As Margaret Mead wrote, 'Never doubt that a small group of thoughtful, committed citizens can change the world; indeed, it's the only thing that ever has.'

For example you might find like-minded friends and have regular meetings to discuss the issues facing us. You might share your hopes and fears. You might look at how to live through disruptions to the food chain, severe weather patterns and an energy crisis. If you have children you might want to explore how you want them to grow up in a world that is dangerous and violent because of starvation, mass migration and mass extinctions. As you plan for a future that will be very different from now you might investigate different scenarios and what your response might be. Maybe you think about selling your separate homes and buying land to create a farming collective. Maybe you decide to take off in a campervan and travel, enjoying the wonders of nature while you still can. Maybe you remain in your current life and enjoy yourself even more because you know soon this will end. Or perhaps you will consciously celebrate life on Earth through music, dance, theatre and art. Humanity has never encountered a catastrophe on this scale or of this kind before. There are no precedents.

Indigenous cultures have known something is dreadfully wrong for a long time but this catastrophe is not of their making and they do not know what to do. No one does. We have to dig deeply into ourselves and find our own way to live through what is coming. Whether with others or alone our love of life will become the ark to carry us through to whatever is our destiny.

I am in my seventies and have moved to Scotland where my husband and I can live the rest of our lives close to nature. Martin has created a community project growing food, running courses for people to learn how to grow vegetables, teaching children in schools to plant seeds, tend crops and care for the environment. I write and walk along lochs and in the mountains, living myself as much as I am able. But we will be dead before the real horror hits. If you are young with your future ahead of you, this is unlikely to be enough for you. You must take action as soon as possible of whatever kind calls you. This book is my contribution to your future and the future of life on Earth.

I'm fed up with following my dreams so decided to ask where they're going and make my own way there.

Chapters

1	The Anthropocene Extinction
2	Building an Ark
3	A Deep Sea Change of Consciousness
4	An Invisible Apocalypse
5	The Dreadful Truth
6	How Have We Got Here?
7	False Hope Is a Form of Denial
8	The Creativity of Love
9	An Age of Extinction
10	The Matrix of Power
11	Losing Our Religion
12	The Sacred Body
13	The Beauty of the Beast
14	The Politics of Experience
15	Divide and Rule
16	The Unconscious Is The Body
17	Maps of Fear
18	The Crazy Wisdom
19	Search for the Wilderness Inside Yourself
20	Releasing the Beast
21	Instinctual Love
22	Instinctual Wisdom
23	Let's Talk About Death
24	Life, Death & the Mystery
25	Eros & Thanatos
26	Life Without Death Would Have No Meaning
27	The Field
28	Fear of Fear
29	Releasing Fear
30	Dimensions of Being
31	A Return to Paradise
32	Love's Body
33	Life and Life in an Eco-Apocalypse.

1   The Anthropocene Extinction

> *We are facing a catastrophe beyond anything the world has seen before. We are well into a Sixth Mass Extinction that will destroy most of life on Earth. The scale of this tragedy is almost impossible to comprehend yet we have to face up to the devastation of what is happening so that we can deal with it intelligently and creatively.*

We are currently living in the Meghalayan age of the Holocene epoch in the Quaternary period of the Cenozoic era of the Phanerozoic eon. There have been three previous aeons, the Hadean, the Archean and the Proterozoic, each with their epochs, ages and periods, and mass extinctions. There have been five previous Mass Extinctions, each wiping out between fifty and ninety-six per cent of all life on Earth. We are now in the middle of a sixth.

This mass extinction is called the Anthropocene Extinction, which means - caused by human activity.

"Earth is experiencing species extinctions, population declines, and massive anthropogenic erosion of biodiversity and the ecosystem to such an extent we are already well into a sixth mass extinction that is severe and irreversible. It is difficult to appreciate that this biological annihilation will be the decimation of the only assemblage of life that we know of in the universe."

Professor G. Ceballos, P. Ehrlich and R Dirzo Proceedings of the National Academy of Science July 2017

The 6th Mass Extinction is a bio-catastrophe almost impossible to comprehend. It is a vast dying on a scale beyond any war or disaster the world has seen before. And while it is the most important and urgent global issue confronting us, we have spectacularly failed to deal with it.

So what if I don't know what Armageddon means - it's not the end of the world.

Global warming, dying oceans, climate chaos, species' extinctions, polluted rivers, deforestation, desertification, biodiversity loss, melting ice-caps, floods, fires, droughts and other dimensions of this eco-Armageddon are apparent all over the world. Yet even though no one will escape the consequences of this eco-crisis, not even the rich and powerful, we seem unable to make the changes necessary to avert it. Politicians talk about how we need urgent action and then delay legislation and set deadlines far in the future. Scientists warn we have just a few years left to change our ways, though many admit we have already left it too late. Campaigners keep saying we are approaching the precipice and must act now; few will speak publicly about what they know in their heart of hearts – we have already gone over that precipice.

At a party talk about global warming - it's a real ice-breaker.

Scientists and people all over the world who have been trying for some time to find ways to live in harmony with nature are now realising we cannot prevent the disintegration of the worldwide food web, the collapse of biodiversity, and the eco-catastrophe of the 6th Mass Extinction. To acknowledge this is painful, frightening and heartbreaking. But false hope is now a form of denial. When we acknowledge the mega-threat we are up against, our responses will be more in line with what is actually possible. The most pressing challenge is no longer about how to avert this crisis; it is how to prepare for it and how to live through it.

'The brutal truth is it is now impossible to stop a full climate breakdown that will wipe out the human race. There isn't going to be any respite. I apologise for being so depressing.' Professor Bill McGuire, Emeritus Professor of Geophysical & Climate Hazards at University College London.

Perhaps you were hoping for the bluebird of happiness – sorry, I'm the bluebottle of despair.

How have we ended up in this catastrophic situation? Why is it so hard for us to collectively and intelligently deal with this global crisis? Most importantly of all, how do we navigate an eco-apocalypse?

It is not enough to merely point at the inactivity of politicians, the capitalist greed of the corporate world, the might of the industrial-military complex or destructive farming and fishing methods. We must make radical changes in the core of our lives. We need a shift in our understanding of what it means to part of the community of life on Earth. Otherwise, in whatever our attempts to live differently, we will recreate the same mistakes that have led to this catastrophe in the first place.

One core problem is the relationship we have with our own bodies. Humans are not only creatures of culture and society; we are also animals. Our animal body keeps us alive. Without it we are nothing. Yet modern culture ignores the essential animal nature of our human-ness and neglects the energy of the body and its instincts. Any animal that neglects its body soon becomes extinct. Which is the void we are staring into, the ultimate oblivion of extinction.

Our collective betrayal and neglect of our own animal-body is reflected in the cruel and calamitous way we treat other animals, so much so we are driving them to extinction too. We need to re-embrace the feeling instincts of the body and let other dimensions than our intellectual minds guide us through the challenges ahead.

I have a lot of compassion but I don't waste it on humans.

Another contributing factor is that we identify ourselves primarily as individuals and value the freedom that gives us more than the responsibilities for community, including responsibility for the community of life on Earth. Each of us is a unique distinct individual yet also part of the interdependent web of life. We have focused on our separate individuality, which gives us freedom, self-determination and a sense of personal worth, but have neglected the interconnectedness with life that sustained and nourished our ancestors.

We need to evolve a greater perspective than just that of us as individuals and re-establish our symbiotic connection with the natural world. This also means acknowledging there is something greater than even humanity – life itself. Not easy for us humans who imagine that because we can name the other animals this renders us superior to them and more important.

Another challenge - the nature of the brilliant human mind itself.

We have separated ourselves from the undifferentiated flow of life that other animals inhabit and become conscious we are alive rather than simply being alive. This alienation from the instinctual flow of life through our bodies has allowed us to develop language, self-awareness and construct complex societies and technologies. It has also led us to denigrate the intelligence of the instincts and pay no heed to the communications from nature warning us we are destroying the very web of life that sustains us.

I ink therefore I am... I think.

Yet another dilemma stems from the same source and one of our greatest strengths - our intellectual and analytical minds and their capacity for abstract and conceptual thought. Such formidable skills enable us to wield great power over life. Unfortunately we have become addicted to that power and in doing so have neglected our equally important vulnerability to life.

This vulnerability is intrinsic to all forms of life as flesh and blood bodies are able to be wounded and die. And because we know death is the annihilation of the individual self, which in modern culture is our identity, we will do almost anything to avoid death. We will even destroy what makes life worth living to live a little longer in a life that is not therefore worth living. Not a good recipe for our stewardship of life on Earth.

At the heart of the eco-crisis lies perhaps the most significant factor of all - we do not love life enough. And here I am not referring to just a love of our own individual lives but a deep love for all living creatures and plants, the rivers, the mountains, the oceans, the fields… all life.

Humanity lives in a perpetual conflict with the realities of life in a body - it's intrinsic vulnerability, its inevitable pain and its ultimate demise. As a consequence we have difficulty embracing life whole-heartedly and with the totality of commitment we see in other animals. Which also means the simple joy of being alive is mostly lost to us in modern culture. Often we have no idea how deeply we love life until it is time to say goodbye on our deathbed. Apart from our existential angst, there are several reasons for this.

One factor is that we are bombarded by images through ads, social media, films etc. of a consumerist version of happiness that teaches us the 'good' life is to be found through owning things - sleek cars, houses with swimming pools, landscaped gardens, exotic holidays, designer clothes, the latest iPhone, and so on - yielding, of course, massive profits for the corporate world.

Yet there is a different kind of happiness that we do not need to seek 'out there' but find within us. To help us navigate the challenges ahead, we need to rediscover the innate natural joy we knew as children and the pure happiness of being alive that lies in our bodies. This will be vitally important when the worldwide food web and our consumerist paradise disintegrate, and the 'good' life as we have known it is gone.

When the grid goes down, we'll be watching Netflix by candlelight.

There are many dimensions to life outside the cultural conditioning of our materialist individualist consumer society. To prepare for the approaching eco-storm we need to reconnect with them. Corporate capitalism, the industrial-military complex, the pollution and unsustainable depletion of the earth's resources and the vested interests of the wealthy and powerful elite have repeatedly resisted the radical changes needed to avert this eco-tragedy. Recently it was revealed that the oil and gas industry has delivered $2.8bn per day in pure profit for the last 50 years totalling $52tn since 1970. (IPCC report, Prof. Aviel Verbruggen) The energy industry will not let this go even for the sake of life on Earth.

Our challenge is no longer how to prevent this crisis, it has become how to navigate it. Let's build our arks.

How about reducing global warming immediately by switching from Fahrenheit to Centigrade!

2 Building an Ark

> *We need to make plans for the coming eco-apocalypse. If we focus only on preventing this eco-Armageddon we will leave it too late to take care of our own lives. We need to build arks to carry us through the dark times ahead in whatever way we feel called to. Whether we create communities or live alone we need to base our lives on different principles than our current society.*

In the film Don't Look Up an asteroid is headed for Earth. Warnings are ignored, scientific fact denied, vested interests dominate, profits matter more than averting the catastrophe, politicians focus on maintaining power rather than the crisis, and most people refuse to face the reality of the devastation heading their way. Sound familiar? The last scene is of friends eating dinner together and spending their last moments loving and caring for each other. When devastation is imminent what else is there?

We may not have reached this point yet but the situation is so dire we need to begin now to think about how to live through the coming devastation. If we can begin to find new ways to deal with what is happening, at least we are giving ourselves a chance.

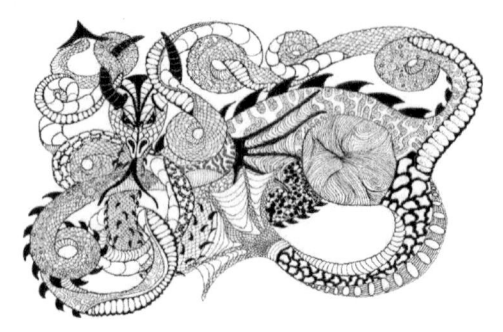

You won't see me coming because I travel at the speed of dark.

We might consider creating self-sufficient communities based on different principles than our current social order. We might grow food in our communities not only in our own private gardens or allotments. We might simply enjoy nature as much as we can while we can. We might follow an urge to leave the city and find a farm sooner than we imagined. We might sit in meditation attuning to the sensations of our bodies and start to trust our instincts more than our thoughts. We might leave our jobs, sell our house and go on the road searching for what we need. We might think far more carefully about bringing children into a world where there will be unforeseen suffering on a scale we cannot yet imagine. We might decide to leave the concerns of the world behind and live deep in nature celebrating the great privilege of being alive on this beautiful planet Earth.

For each of us our path will be different.

I think I'll die early to avoid the rush.

Even if it is too late to prevent this eco-catastrophe we can explore how to live through it and create as good a life as possible. For a start, when we listen to the ancient instinctual wisdom in our bodies with aeons of evolution behind it to ensure our survival, we will be more attuned to finding a way forward.

This subtle listening involves a return to our roots as animals with different priorities than our culturally conditioned ideas and beliefs. The good life for an animal is simply the freedom to enjoy being alive and one thing we can do immediately is bring back into our lives the natural joy that lives in our bodies. This will lead us into a new relationship with life and connect us with a different kind of happiness than material wealth, one where experience is more important than owning things.

As well as pursuing happiness 'out there' we will discover a more innocent happiness 'in here', within our bodies, the kind of happiness we knew as children before we were taught that making money and climbing the corporate ladder are far more important. This will also lead us into a renewed respect for the animal body and the body of life itself. A love of life itself will then be at the heart of how we live.

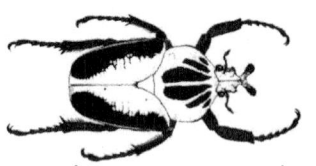

I can be anyone I want to be.   Isn't that identity theft?

Whether we decide to live as consciously as we can within our current lives or take the route of creating new communities, we cannot just continue the old social order and cultural mores of our current society. We need to make radical changes to how we live in almost all areas of our lives.

We especially need to reconnect with aspects of our humanity that have been abandoned in our long flight away from the animal.

Among other changes, this realignment with our deeper humanity will connect us with what we truly need rather than what we think we want. We can then do our best to create a life that honours the energy of our bodies. And our natural selves are very different from the culturally created egos fostered by a society that wants us to be consumers rather than free individuals who threaten the current social order with our self-determination.

The old political, economic, cultural and religious structures and institutions are going to be swept away in the anarchy of the eco disasters being unleashed anyway. The sooner we find new ways of being human and living together with each other and the rest of life on this planet, the better. Get together with friends. Speak about the future. Plan now for what is going to hit us far sooner than anyone expected. Meditate. Wander off the beaten track into wilderness or stay grounded in your current life until shown otherwise.

But whatever your route, listen to your instincts not only your intellect, tune into the wisdom of the body not only the mind. Good luck everybody – we're going to need it!

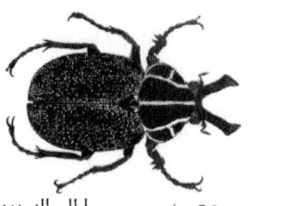

We'll all be gone in 50 years.

OMG! What did you say!

We'll all be gone in 50 years.

Phew - I thought you said 15!

3   A Deep Sea Change of Consciousness

> *There are many ways to prepare for the crisis ahead such as to create farming communities, learn natural medicine, teach children to grow food, practise survival skills and learn how to cook and build from basic materials. Here we are exploring the change needed in our psycho-spiritual relationship with the natural environment and our own animal nature.*

So many anti-life dynamics are systemically entrenched within the human mind and the matrix of modern politics, economics, culture and religion, it seems only a shock can now precipitate action. If we had been willing to make the changes needed we would have done so long ago. Unfortunately the world is in denial that the devastating force of the Anthropocene Extinction is not only irreversible, it has already begun.

What you most need is often hidden behind what you least want.

The idea that we can prevent this cascading Armageddon if we recycle plastic, drive electric cars and sign online petitions is a delusion – but an understandable one. Many people have enough on ensuring they have sufficient shelter, food and heating without contemplating how dreadful the future looks. But when the devastating reality hits us in floods, drought, starvation, fires, desertification, mass migrations, however we experience it, our hearts will break. Not only at the loss of our livelihoods and homes, when we see what we have done to life on this beautiful Earth. We have destroyed it.

Maybe it is too painful to face yet and only when the full reality hits will we make the fundamental changes necessary. Let's hope we do not leave it until it is too late.

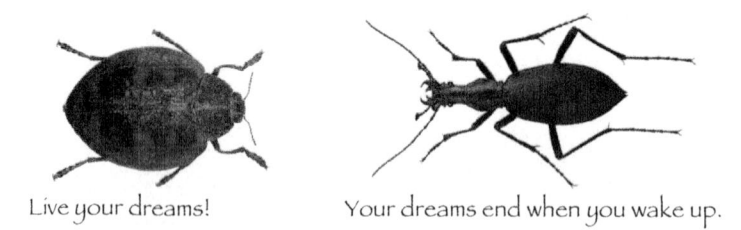

Live your dreams!   Your dreams end when you wake up.

Though the reality is, it is already too late. Back in 1948 we could have paid heed to Fairfield Osborn in his book *Our Plundered Planet*, where he warned we were turning Earth into a desert with our poor stewardship of the land and William Vogt when he warned us of the dangers of deforestation and overpopulation in his *Road to Survival*.

We could have listened to Rachel Carson sixty years ago when she wrote in *Silent Spring*, 'We stand where two roads diverge. The road we have been travelling is a smooth superhighway on which we progress with speed, but at the end lies disaster. The other fork of the road, the road less travelled, offers our last and only chance to reach a destination that assures the preservation of the earth.'

We could have listened to the 'back to the land' eco-hippies in the 1970s who tried to grow food on self-sufficient farms in harmony with nature. We could have listened to the demands for environmental justice in the 1980s. In 1992 we could have paid heed to the warnings of The UN Earth Summit in Rio de Janeiro. In 2006 we could have woken up to the facts in Al Gore's documentary *An Inconvenient Truth*.

Many of us on the ground were increasingly realising the true nature of this catastrophe but those in power didn't listen to any of it. This deafness has continued. As I write not a single agreement signed at Cop26 has been implemented.

The French aristocracy didn't see it coming either.

The full effects of ignoring these warnings may not be apparent yet. In wealthy industrialised nations, the shelves in supermarkets are still piled high with food, we can drink the water coming from our taps, and even if increasingly expensive we can still watch TV in warm homes. It is hard to see the fragility of the food chain and the infrastructures of society that we take for granted. However many countries are already experiencing this crisis - Afghanistan, Bangladesh, Chad, Haiti, Kenya, Malawi, Niger, Pakistan, Somalia and Sudan, to name a few.

These countries have not caused this crisis yet they are struggling on the front line of climate breakdown. We should be doing all we can to help them. Yet rich nations are utterly failing to provide the assistance needed to poorer nations who are suffering from what is our responsibility.

Last year, the UK slashed overseas aid by nearly 30%, an appalling decision. Yet when ecological collapse bites even deeper, even industrialised communities will experience systemic and environmental breakdown. Starvation, violence and terror will follow. If we are not prepared, the mass hysteria and panic will engulf us too. The challenge is no longer how to prevent this eco-catastrophe, it has become how to prepare for it and live through it as best we can. For this we need to start our preparations now.

Wow! This global warming is happening far more quickly than I realised.

It's Spring you idiot.

The individualistic isolation of nuclear families with their own washing machines and heating, where we each do our own shopping and cooking, provides a ready-made market and suits capitalist consumerism very well. But this is going to end. We will need each other more than we ever imagined. For example we may need to create new communities, based on radically different principles, of whatever kind serves us. Exactly what we do and how we arrange things will be according to our particular inclinations and needs.

Though one thing is certain - no one is going to organise this for us. Politicians, transnational corporations, the industrial and military complex, pharmaceutical companies, the oil and gas energy empires and the rich and privileged elites are too invested in the current status quo. We have to organise and get together whatever we need for ourselves and come together in ways that transcend old inequalities, whatever the cultural, political, economic or historical differences and injustices that threaten to divide us. When your house is burning you save lives first and can argue about the pains of history later if you need to.

You should turn your lights off to save energy

I did that once and ran over a a ladybird in the dark.

31

Without a radical shift in consciousness that puts aside the personal politics of difference, we will re-create in new communities the same divisive power dynamics that contributed to this bio-catastrophe. The common ground that stands under us all is the earth beneath our feet, whatever our race, nationality, gender, colour, religion or shoe size and whether our skills are as farmers, healers, mechanics, poets, teachers, mystics, musicians, cooks, builders or horse-whisperers. This itself is under threat.

Soil is a biological structure, continually created and renewed by the organisms that inhabit it. When conditions become hostile to the survival of these organisms, the structure of the soil collapses, and fertile lands turn to deserts. The global rate of soil degradation is terrifying. 33% is already degraded and over 90% is predicted to be degraded by 2050 (FAO and ITPS, 2015; IPBES, 2018) We rely on the soil for 95% of our food yet the equivalent of one football pitch is being eroded every five seconds. Soil can be worth more than what grows in it yet we treat it like dirt.

Someone keeps dumping soil on my allotment. The plot thickens.

Prof Antonelli, the director of science at the Royal Botanical Gardens, Kew, led research involving 210 scientists from 42 countries. They discovered that 40% of the world's plant species are at risk of extinction within 30 years as a result of desertification and the destruction of the natural world.

Whatever common ground unites us, we each bring different skills and abilities to the challenges of this eco-crisis. For some their response will be to create self-sufficient farming communities. For others it might be to work within current social and political systems to create sustainable forms of energy and eco-technologies. Some might campaign and demonstrate, others might continue in their current lives while preparing various escape routes. Some may teach children the lost arts of herbal medicine, cooking, survival skills, vegetable growing and animal husbandry.

Others might celebrate the magnificence of life in dance, music, theatre and sport, others in long walks in mountains or swimming in lochs. Some may feel called to create a deep-sea change of consciousness within the geo-soul of the collective psyche. I am exploring here the work required in the inner realms, a transformation of human consciousness.

Are we paddling our own canoe or all in the same boat?

No idea but I'm learning how to swim.

4   An Invisible Apocalypse

> *We need a different kind of hope, one that is not only about how to prevent this catastrophe, as this is no longer possible, but also about how to navigate it. We need to understand that inner dynamics within our psyches have also contributed to this apocalyptic nightmare. And we need a radical shift in human consciousness so profound it changes our understanding of what it means to be alive.*

The Millennium Ecosystem Assessment, which involved more than a thousand experts, estimated an extinction rate of up to 8,700 species a year, or 24 a day. More recently, scientists at the U.N. Convention on Biological Diversity concluded: 'Every day, up to 150 species are lost.' That could be as much as 10% a decade.

We can no longer prevent these dreadful losses. A techno-utopianism that imagines either science or a sudden change in political will is going to miraculously save us has shown itself to be a dead-end. We are staring into a profoundly dystopian future. Climate chaos, pollution, starvation, antibiotic resistant diseases, the collapse of biodiversity and the disintegration of the world-wide food web are going to wipe out our global civilisation and drive most species of animals and plants, including ourselves, into the ultimate death that is extinction.

The situation is so dire it is hard to think or read about it because the facts are so devastating.

There's not enough food and too many people.

Have they considered cannibalism?

Yet we need hope, otherwise we fall into despair. On reading what I've written one friend said, if you describe the undiluted reality people will just switch off and go shopping. Another told me a helpless paralysis came over them. But as the facts reveal themselves, old hopes fade.

We tend to think there is no other option than to keep fighting with hope and determination to save the natural world from this destruction. Of course we must do what we can. Even when we know we cannot change the ultimate outcome, our actions have intrinsic worth. They are expressions of our love for life. Yet we need a different kind of hope, one that is not just about how to prevent this catastrophe but about how to navigate it.

If ignorance is bliss why aren't more people happy?

Most focus has inevitably been on external aspects of this crisis — of course, this is the destruction of what literally matters, the natural world. But there are other dimensions, equally important.

The human intellectual mind, our conscious awareness, the inner dynamics of our psyches, the subtle energies of our feeling bodies, the ingenuity and resourcefulness of the human spirit that creates beauty, wisdom and understanding out of our experience, these are also involved in the unfolding eco-crisis.

There is a synergy between our inner and outer worlds in which each reflects the other. We need to explore the psycho-spiritual dimensions of this eco-crisis as they too have played their part in its creation and will be vital for our navigation through it.

For example: The intellectual mind thinks it is cleverer than the sensitivities and intelligence of the instincts. Unresolved fears of our vulnerable mortality drive us to relentlessly seek power and control over life. The collective world-ego is addicted to the material world and seeks happiness through owning things. Humanity's fear of death leads us to sacrifice life in order merely to survive. Religions steal the life and love belonging to the animal body and give it to an artificially created idea of a soul, then preach an after-life is more important than this life.

These aspects of humanity are as much a source of the eco-crisis as the industrial-military complex, corporate greed and the ruthless pursuit of profit. We have to find a new way of being.

I'm on my 4th guardian angel - the 1st had a breakdown, the 2nd is in therapy, and the 3rd applied for a transfer to another planet.

Alongside working to find new ways to alleviate our destruction of the natural world through economic, environmental and political action, we also need to explore our inner worlds. This is in order to uncover new dimensions of our humanity that are not alienated from life but deeply aligned with it.

I was born in Northampton, a city in the middle of England, in 1949. I remember being woken up by birds singing their dawn chorus, even in our cobbled streets with terraced houses and tiny gardens. In summer we had to close the windows if the lights were on because thousands of moths, daddy long-legs and flying insects would fling themselves at the glass. Every street lamp was surrounded by hundreds of moths. Car windscreens were covered with squashed insects. In the mornings spiders' webs sparkled with dew in all directions across paths and between bushes. Worms, beetles, ladybirds, ants, bees, wasps, flies, dragonflies were everywhere in abundance. But we never fully appreciated the glorious bird song nor wondered at the magnificence of the insects. We took them for granted. For those who remember what it used to be like, this loss is a tragic reminder of how much we loved these creatures but didn't realise it until too late.

When I was young the Dead Sea was just sick.

Inger Andersen, the executive director of the UN Environment Programme (UNEP), said recently, 'We had our chance to make incremental changes, but that time is over. Only a root-and-branch transformation of our economies and societies can save us from accelerating climate disaster.' The UN's environment agency aso recently announced, 'There is no credible pathway to 1.5C in place, and the failure to reduce carbon emissions means the only way to limit the worst impacts of the climate crisis is a rapid transformation of societies.'

We not only need radical changes to our culture and behaviour, we need a shift in consciousness so profound it changes our understanding of what it means to be human. We need to reconnect with the deep instinctive love of life buried in our bodies. We need to reawaken to our animal nature and realise the other animals are not alien to us, they are our kin. We need to allow the intelligence of our instincts to inform us of what we truly need rather than what we think we want. And we need the inner dimensions of our conscious awareness and the creativity of our human spirit to help us in our quest to find a way through this cataclysmic eco-apocalypse.

With these shifts to our understanding and consciousness, we can live through the dark times ahead in ways that foster understanding, meaning, freedom, beauty, truth, wisdom, love and other creations of the human spirit. All of which creates a legacy for future life. This is not about only our own survival; it is about something far more important. It is about the future of life on Earth.

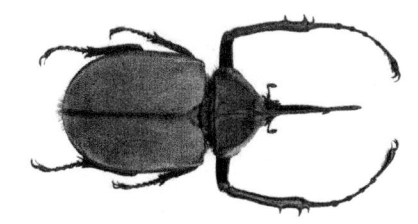

Please don't destroy the planet –
where would I keep my twig collection?

Though to create a future grounded in reality, we must face what is actually happening – despite that it is so devastating and heartbreaking.

5   The Dreadful Truth

> *Despite knowing for some time the extensive and dangerous harm we have been doing to the natural world, we have been unable to change. Even now, when we know we are headed for absolute disaster, we still seem unable to prevent the behaviour that is causing this eco-Armageddon. We seem to be engaged in a war on life itself.*

Over 50 years ago, the astronauts on Apollo 8 saw Earth rising over the horizon of the moon. It was the only colour in a vast darkness. They said it looked so beautiful yet so alone they wept. The pictures they sent back to Earth then revealed to us all that humans, plants and animals share a unique planetary home. We also became aware that Earth does not extend boundlessly in all directions, it is finite and needs our care.

It's a small world but I wouldn't want to lick it clean every day.

Since then, the devastation we have unleashed on the natural world has increased phenomenally.

We know that the destruction of the rainforest, bottom trawling fishing, toxic pollution, overpopulation, factory farming, pesticides, fossil fuels and unsustainable use of land, water and energy has led to the mass dying of animals, plants and fungi, yet we have done nothing of significance to avert the catastrophe of the Sixth Mass Extinction now upon us.

The first Earth Summit was in Rio de Janeiro in 1992. It was full of optimism and hope. Twenty years later another summit was held, Rio+20. Every environmental problem identified at the original Earth Summit had become worse, often very much worse, with no sign of this cataclysmic destruction changing. This inaction has continued.

Leading conservationists have condemned nature protection efforts as a 'massive failure'. They suggest we embrace this failure because the only way to get anything done is when people actually experience the devastation unleashed. Though they also say by then it will be too late. As I write, not a single country has honoured the promises made last year at Cop 26 in Glasgow and the world has not met any of the twenty biodiversity targets set by global governments a decade ago.

No matter where you look you always face the consequences.

'Humanity is in the danger zone. No nation is immune. We have a choice. Collective action or collective suicide. Yet we continue to feed our fossil fuel addiction - which is suicide.' António Guterres, the UN secretary general.

It is not only fossil fuels and global warming. The Environment Agency published their annual report in 2020 on the state of rivers in England. Every single river and lake in England without exception is polluted beyond EU legal limits. Raw sewage, fertilisers, pesticides, toxic chemicals and hazardous substances are disgorged or seep insidiously into our rivers continually. And that is just the stuff we know about. Nanomaterials, microplastics and pharmaceuticals also flow through our rivers with a raft of unknown consequences. Meanwhile Defra has slashed the Environment Agency's budget to the point its own officers say that 'Defra's river monitoring is 'not fit for purpose', 'useless', 'unscientific', and' a waste of money'. Which raises the question: could the true picture be even worse? (*How clean are England's rivers?* Rachel Salvidge, Guardian Sep 2020)

Rivers are a country's life-blood. England is now a country where you cannot swim in any river or lake without endangering your health. Millions of creatures and plants are dying because of this endemic toxic pollution. England has poisoned itself. The response of the Environment Agency to this situation? *'Now we have left the EU we can change the law so that existing water quality rules can be tweaked to see more rivers classed in good health.'* Sir James Bevan, CEO of the Environment Agency.

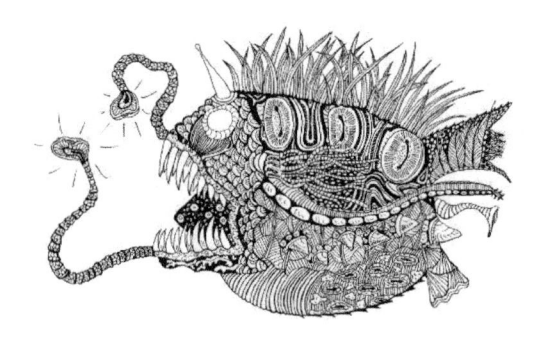

But what if you see an endangered animal eating an endangered plant?

Another example: The agreement to halt global deforestation, signed by Brazil and others at Cop26, was hailed as a big 'win'. Since then Brazil's deforestation rate has soared to record levels. According to data from national space research agency Inpe, the first four months of 2022 saw an increase in 69% of rainforest destruction compared to the same period in 2021. In April 2022, 1,012.5 square km of Brazilian rainforest, an area greater than the size of New York, was lost to deforestation. There is no sign of this catastrophic destruction lessening.

30th June 2022, the Supreme Court in the US made a devastating decision. It ruled in favour of a lawsuit brought by fossil-fuel-producing states against the Environmental Protection Agency (EPA). This decision strips power from regulatory agencies and prevents the use of the Clean Air Act to phase out fossil fuel power plants. As a result, it is impossible for the US to achieve its goal of halving greenhouse gas emissions by 2030. Which anyway in light of recent climate disasters is generally agreed by climate scientists to be dangerously too low.

'We are a plague on the Earth.' David Attenborough

I've just watched a terrifying horror movie!

I hate to break it to you sister - that was the news.

Not only are we collectively failing to do anything significant to avert this eco-apocalypse, we seem to have become bio-terrorists actively seeking to destroy life on Earth. World War III has arrived. And it is a war on life itself.

'I don't know what World War III will look like but World War IV will be fought with sticks and stones.' Albert Einstein

There will be no more wars where we are headed. Not because we have raised our consciousness to such a level we no longer have wars and a deep peace has broken out, because there will be no more humans and very few animals, plants and fungi left to fight, breathe, procreate, eat, play, creep, crawl, swim, fly, climb, run and do anything anywhere. Most will be dead. Even the depths of the oceans are becoming dead zones, polluted beyond repair in this current Anthropocene Extinction Event.

How on earth have we ended up here?

What if when you die God asks: So, how was heaven?

6   How Have We Got Here?

> *It is difficult to understand that we've left it too late to reverse this eco-catastrophe. This is because the very nature of our human mind and consciousness has led us into this crisis. We do not know another way to go about things.*

The four horsemen of the eco-Apocalypse:
- The vast international industrial-military complex.
- Corporate greed and mass consumerism.
- The human global super-predator.
- The human mind and its addiction to power.

The deeper grammar generating these and our totally inadequate response to the eco-crisis they have created lies in the very core of our humanity. The evolution of the human mind and the development of self-awareness necessitated an alienation from our natural animal selves. Only a creature divided from itself can turn around and look at itself and know itself. Our dislocation from our instinctual nature is the source of our consciousness and culture yet is also at the heart of the tragedy now unfolding in the natural world.

If this world isn't driving you crazy you must be insane.

This cultural divorce from our animal-ness has also led to our spectacular success as a species. Our brilliant minds have created technologies and understandings that have revolutionised our lives. The average life expectancy in the Middle Ages in Europe was 30 years; it is now over 80. Children now survive the dangers that killed most children in the past. We have pharmaceutical drugs and medical technologies that cure diseases that would have led to death in previous times. We have developed intensive farming methods that mean we eat a varied diet throughout the year. We have created technologies of power and energy that mean we no longer suffer as our ancestors did in a continual battle to keep warm and survive.

Our technological prowess is phenomenal. And the seeds of this eco-catastrophe lie right in the heart of our success. The human global population has expanded exponentially, we have consumed vast natural resources, and we have developed powerful weapons capable of destroying life on Earth.

'The world's 7.6 billion people represent just 0.01% of all living things, yet humanity has caused the loss of 83% of all wild mammals and half of all plants.' Yinon M. Bar-On, Rob Phillips, and Ron Milo, Proceedings of National Academy of Sciences 2018

You've got to get this stuff into historical perspective.

But history now isn't what it was.

It is natural to fight to defend ourselves, to develop weapons to protect our families, to construct technologies that give us power over what happens. Every species has their way of going about these things. On a planet where 'kill or be killed' is the Law of the Jungle, anything without defences against being eaten would have become extinct long ago. Yet the powers of other animals, such as sharp claws, stings, strong teeth and poisonous venom, evolved in tandem with instincts and strategies for survival that maintained the biodiversity and homeostasis of the whole ecosystem. We humans have developed technologies that can destroy the Earth several times over in one generation, far too quickly to have evolved the capacity to use such power wisely.

I see humans have developed nuclear weapons - perhaps they're more intelligent than we thought.

I doubt it. They've got them all pointed at each other.

Our brilliant human minds have made scientific discoveries and created technologies that have built a global infrastructure of fantastic complexity with phenomenal reach. These mega-technologies are powerful beyond our capacity to use them wisely and we have ended up with a monstrous killing machine.

We have hunted species to extinction, laid waste to vast areas of the environment, plundered the Earth's resources, farmed with pesticides and cruelty, cut down the rainforest, polluted rivers and overfished oceans until the forests, rivers and oceans are themselves dying.

We have developed weapons of war such as nuclear submarines that can launch missiles to destroy over 200 cities anywhere in the world in less time than it takes to order and take delivery of a pizza. We have enough thermo-nuclear warheads, intercontinental missiles, bio-weapons, chimera viruses, Thermobaric Bombs and Hydrogen Bombs to destroy the global eco-system and pretty much everything alive several times over. Humanity has become a 'global super-predator'.

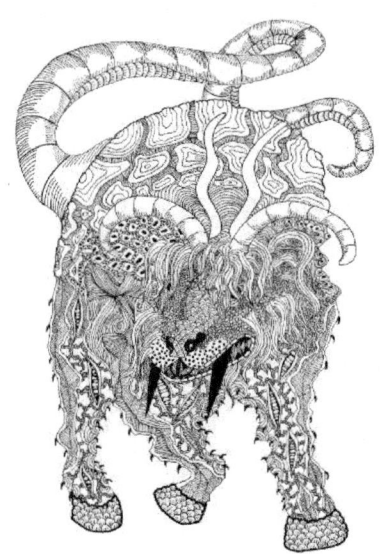

When you're good, you have few enemies –
when you're ruthless you have none.

A super-predator overhunts populations of animals so they cannot replenish their numbers, like the herds of elephants machine-gunned down from helicopters for their ivory and the killing of adult apex carnivores such as bears, wolves and lions for sport. In the US more than 100 million animals are killed by hunters each year. That number does not include the millions of animals for which kill figures are not maintained by state wildlife agencies. Over 4,000 tons of lead are shot into the environment by those hunters leading to another estimated 20 million animals dying from lead poisoning. A vast killing for 'fun' not food.

As a result of humanity's ignorance and greed, animals are now dying at nine times the rate they can reproduce. In the last 50 years we have lost 68% of all vertebrates. 60% of all mammals are now livestock, 36% are human, only 4% are wild.

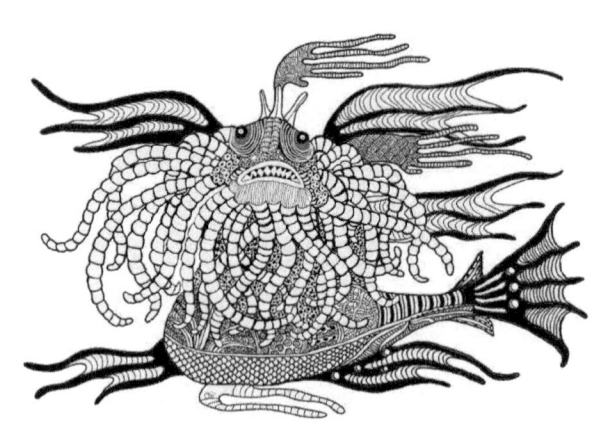

I leave you in peace - you leave me in pieces.

There are many responses to this dire situation. Some create new technologies to generate clean recyclable energy, clear the oceans of plastic and build electric cars. Some turn back to the land to live in the simpler ways of our ancestors. Many have become vegetarian and tried to decrease their carbon footprint by buying less. Yet even all of these together are not enough to avert the approaching global catastrophe. The reality now is we cannot avoid impending disaster. This is not an inconvenient truth; it is an utterly devastating truth.

OMG! When the eco-apocalypse hits and the grid goes down - I won't be able to charge my phone!

7 False Hope Is a Form Of Denial

> *The mass extinction of so many species will soon force us to realise, we love life more than money and power even though we did not recognise this until too late. This love helps us understand though our world will be destroyed, life itself will continue. And this matters. Death is part of the mystery through which life renews itself and renders life precious and meaningful.*

You may think, why keep banging on about how dire the situation is, it doesn't help. But the majority of people do not know and do not want to know how dreadful the eco-crisis actually is. Many commentators and campaigners who know the reality are afraid to share the actual level of devastation already underway. They want to encourage people to take action and know dire warnings of apocalyptic doom can send people out shopping or into despair.

I never argue about global warming, things get too heated.

David Attenborough said that even as a young man he could see that 'the forests and seas were already emptying.' He hoped to create change to the way we lived by opening people's eyes to the wonder and magnificence of the natural world. He says he now regrets not being more honest about the real situation much earlier.

'*It is very hard to get used to the idea that climate catastrophe, far from being imminent, has already taken place. The end has already occurred. How to navigate the broken waters of the catastrophe that has already happened?*'
Timothy Morton, Dark Ecology

If you keep calm and carry on,
you haven't understood what's happening.

A group of 17 internationally renowned scientists reported their findings of over ten years in Frontiers in Conservation Science, 2020. They wrote, '*The Earth is facing a ghastly future of mass extinction yet people still haven't grasped the urgency of the biodiversity and climate crises.*' One of them, Prof Paul Ehrlich from Stanford University, said they were all shocked by what they found. '*We have discovered the planet is in a much worse state than most people – even scientists – understood. The scale of the threats to the biosphere and all its life forms – including humanity – is in fact so great that it is difficult to grasp for even well-informed experts.*'

This report came months after the world failed to meet any of the UN biodiversity targets created to stem the destruction of the natural world. Not one of the 20 goals had been reached. This is the second consecutive time governments have failed to meet a single one of their 10-year biodiversity goals.

'We're doomed. The outcome is death. It is the end of most life on the planet. I am not going to write anymore because there is nothing more can be said.' Mayer Hillman, Senior Fellow Emeritus, Policy Studies Institute.

It's always darkest just before it goes pitch black.

So many studies have revealed the dreadful reality of the Anthropocene Extinction, and so much information is out there and freely available, anyone who genuinely wants to know is already aware of this unfolding catastrophe. Many look away because it is too overwhelming to contemplate the full horror of such an apocalyptic nightmare. Others live in hope that protests and direct action can somehow save us. Others bury their heads in a techno-utopianism that imagines science and technology will save the day. Unfortunately false hope is now a form of denial.

'Nothing fundamental needs to change, we can sit and wait for technological and demographic shifts and everything will work out in the end. A simple story with a happy ending, telling power what it wants to hear, this is the Disney version of environmental science.' George Monbiot

The mass extinction will not be televised.

Many of us have gone through heartbreak and despair as we realised sooner than we ever imagined, we'll be witnessing the end of our human culture and the extinction of most of life on Earth. We now hope to navigate this eco-tragedy with a different kind of activism. Alongside trying to survive this crisis we also need to find meaning, love, beauty, dignity, truth, freedom, understanding, whatever creations of the human spirit we are attuned to, in this unfolding catastrophe. But first we must face the profundity of the loss. It will break our hearts. Then we have to dig deep to find a different kind of hope and meaning.

Never give up on your dreams.    *No, that's why I sleep all the time.*

8   The Creativity of Love

> *The tragedy of the eco-catastrophe will reveal how much we love life more than money, power or status. This love can become a creative force in our lives that shows us a new way of being.*

Many say we must not give up hope, we must be positive, to fall into despair is wrong and an abandonment of the situation, we must keep on fighting. But to find anything meaningful in this tragic scenario we must face the reality that this really is the very worst that could be happening and there is no point pretending otherwise. There is more creative wisdom to be found in experiencing reality, however painful and heartbreaking, than being comforted by ungrounded hopes and dreams, however seductive and full of false promise.

They told me I was delusional so I jumped on my unicorn, spread my wings and flew over the rainbow.

When someone is dying, they, their family and the medical team do all they can to keep them alive. Gradually it becomes apparent death is inevitable. The medical team usually realise this first, then the one dying, only near the end the family. The death void we are staring into now is the end of our world. Some already know this tragedy cannot now be averted; most do not. Though soon everyone will and panic, despair, impotent rage and violence will arise all over the world.

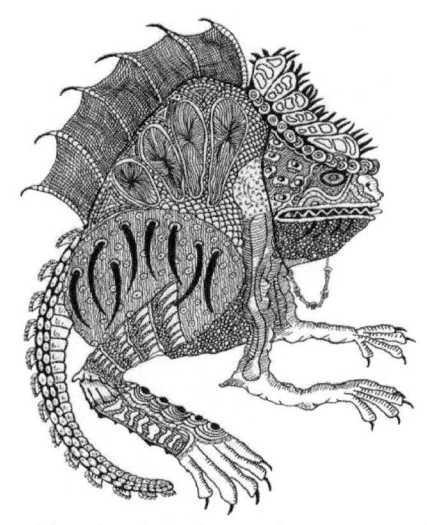

Perhaps I should meditate, it's better than sitting and doing nothing.

Yet facing the reality of the approaching apocalypse does not mean nihilistic despair. By encountering tragedy with an open heart we can create something meaningful. The ancient Greeks understood tragedy was not to be avoided. Aristotle wrote, 'tragedy cleanses the heart through pity and terror, purging us of our petty concerns and worries.' Perhaps we need some of that old wisdom to help us now.

But first we have to see this dreadful situation as it really is and that there is no more of the old hope. This means we will feel grief, anger, sadness and heartbreak. But on the other side of despair we can find a new kind of hope and a different kind of activism becomes possible.

Alongside whatever we need to do to alleviate the destructive harm of the eco-crisis the human spirit can create something meaningful from the tragedy. Sometimes the triumph is in the consciousness created by the experience. Sometimes it's in the laughter at the insanity of it all. Sometimes it's simply the love in the tears we weep. The creativity of the human spirit, despite our tragic collective failure to avert tragedy, will find ways to create consciousness, meaning, laughter and love out of this cataclysmic tragedy. At least some of us will. We can then bequeath this as our legacy to future generations of life. This matters because although we are witnessing the end of our world, it is not the end of life. Life itself will continue.

The snow must go on!

All life dies. Death is part of the mystery through which life continually renews itself. This mass extinction is not therefore the end of life. Life will continue on Earth until the Earth itself dies. Who knows what might be happening on a planet in a galaxy far, far away. And death is as potent as life.

Death brings into sharp focus how precious life is. Death reveals how life itself is more important than our individual survival. Death makes apparent how profoundly we love life even when we do not realise it until it is too late, on our death bed and time to say goodbye. These understandings, together with the conscious awareness of life they engender, can form part of our legacy to future life.

Facing the horrors of a Mass Extinction can bring to our consciousness a love of life that transcends mere survival. This extended love gives meaning to life beyond our own lives and contributes to the energy fields of existence. The evolution of this love is perhaps a vital aspect of our destiny, part of the evolution of a mystery beyond our comprehension.

Maybe life itself is creating the love that, outside the dimensions of space and time, brought inanimate matter to life in the first place. Some force did - why not love? Look around at the world about us - it all had its primary source in birds and bees, mammals and reptiles, flowers and trees, men and women coming together to make new life, making love. In which case let's fulfil our destiny and love life to the full while we still can – and love life enough to die for it.

'If you have nothing you're willing to die for, then you are not fit to live.'
Malcolm X

Only the young die good.

9   An Age of Extinction

> *Mass extinctions are part of the history of life on Earth. Each extinction event allowed new forms of life to evolve. But whatever the future for life, many dimensions of human society and culture will be gone forever. The loss and heartbreak will shift our understanding of what it means to be human.*

More than 99% of all organisms that have ever lived on Earth are extinct. As new species evolve to fit ever changing environments, older species die out. But the rate of extinction varies. There have been times when 75% to 96% of all species disappeared relatively quickly in catastrophic mass extinctions. According to scientists, global extinctions come roughly every 27 million years, which means Earth is overdue a mass extinction by 30 million years.

The most catastrophic mass extinction was 252 million years ago, the P-T extinction known as the 'Great Dying'. 96% of all marine species and about three of every four species on land were exterminated. Marine ecosystems took four to eight million years to recover. The world's forests were wiped out and didn't return until about 10 million years later. It took even longer for living, breathing organisms to return.

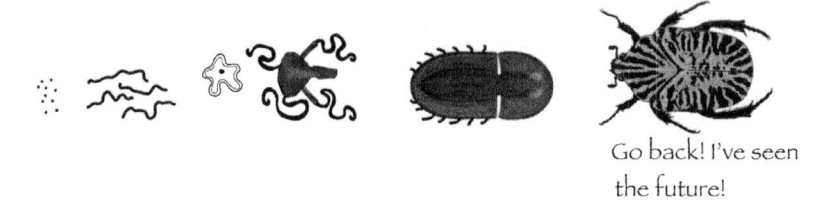

Go back! I've seen the future!

The last mass extinction, the K-T extinction event, was 65 million years ago. This was caused by an asteroid 15 km wide crashing into what is now Mexico at such a high velocity it vaporised. The force of the impact threw huge amounts of debris into the air and caused massive tidal waves to wash over the American continents. Substantial fires broke out. A huge blast wave and heatwave threw vast amounts of material up into the atmosphere that travelled all around the world and blocked out the Sun. Plant growth was stunted, herbivores starved, carnivores in turn starved, and the whole ecosystem collapsed. All life, from microorganisms through to dinosaurs, was affected.

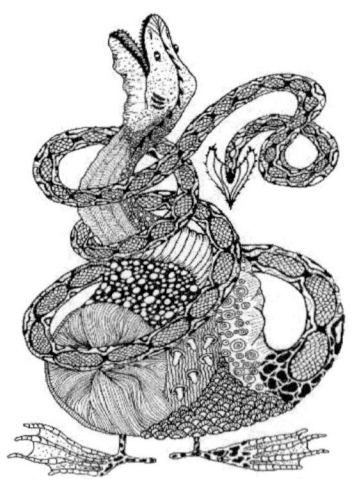

I wondered why that meteorite was getting bigger and bigger – then it hit me.

The asteroid was an exceptional cause of a mass extinction, most have been driven by changes to the Earth's carbon cycle involving large volcanic eruptions. These ejected vast amounts of heat-trapping gases into the atmosphere leading to global warming, ocean acidification and anoxia, the loss of dissolved oxygen in water, which is exactly what is happening with the current global warming.

Though the current mass extinction is not due to movements of the Earth's tectonic plates and an eruption from the Earth's core, nor to an asteroid hitting us from outer space; it is an Anthropocene Extinction, meaning created by human activity.

The last mass extinction led to the end of the dinosaurs and many other species but it also paved the way for mammals and birds to diversify and evolve. In the same way, this may be the end time of our Holocene epoch when mammals ruled the world but it is not the end of life on Earth. The Anthropocene extinction will give space and freedom for other life forms to evolve. Maybe the next era will be the age of the insects, fungi or deep-sea Loricifera and mud dragons. We'll never know.

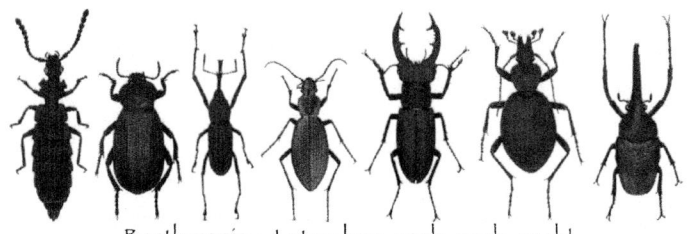

Beetlemania – Let us bee, yeah, yeah, yeah!

However you look at it, and whatever might be the cosmic meaning of it all, this Mass Extinction is the end of our world, the world we have created over millions of years since before the Stone Age. The creations and wonders of humanity, our art, philosophy, culture, music, feasts, schools, knowledge, songs, literature, medicine, technology, architecture, libraries, hospitals, millennia of human endeavour, creativity and understanding… all will be gone. Together with the trillions of animals, plants, fungi and microorganisms we're taking down with us, all of us lost forever into the ultimate death that is extinction.

Help! I can't stop thinking like this!

Yet an event is never truly over; it lives on in unfolding futures forever. We will live on in future life on Earth, until the Earth itself dies, until this universe dies. But whatever the long-term future for existence, the tragic reality here and now is that we are living through a vast mass dying.

As the painful reality becomes increasingly apparent, we will all go through a period of mourning and grief for the life we have lost. Which will break our hearts open to how much we loved life but didn't realise until it was too late.

As we race towards Earth system collapse, trying to raise the alarm feels like being trapped behind a thick plate of glass. As we frantically bang the glass, we look ever crazier. And feel it. I've been working on these issues since I was 22, and full of confidence and hope. I'm about to turn 59, and the confidence is turning to cold fear, the hope to horror. It becomes ever harder to know how to hold it together. I cry most days now.' George Monbiot Guardian Jan 2022

Que sera, sera, what will be will be.   Stop being so stark raving calm!

To navigate the dark future ahead requires more fundamental strategies than we've tried so far. We need a radical revolution in the collective geo-socio-psycho-spiritual body politic, one that leads to a new way of being and changes our understanding of what it means to be a human being.

The destruction and death of so much will anyway soon force the collective ego of the world to experience the full consequences of what we have done to life on Earth. This will be so catastrophic there will be no escaping reality through denial or false hope. In the face of the reality of this bio-apocalyptic nightmare, a radical shift in human consciousness offers a different kind of hope.

I would be a radical activist and start a revolution - but I've just bought a cushion.

What dimensions of our experience and consciousness need to be changed in order to discover this new way of being?

10   The Matrix of Power

> *The eco-crisis has many roots in our culture and society. A focus on the rights of the individual more than the responsibilities of community has led to deep imbalances within society. Global injustice and entrenched privilege have created inequalities of wealth and power that harm our collective co-existence. Our addiction to seeking happiness through owning things has led to a soulless materialism and a greedy plunder of the Earth's resources.*

The human mind and its collective body politic is an immense complexity. It constitutes the most powerful entity on the planet. Only the Earth itself is more powerful. This makes it difficult to understand that science and technology will not save us. The brilliant human intellectual mind does not hold the answers this time. In this crisis, the techno-utopianism of the scientific world is an illusion. There are several reasons for this.

The industrial-military complex and pharmaceutical companies fund much, if not most, scientific research. As a result we have amazing weaponry, can fly into space, and have extended life expectancy fantastically, but in the process have destroyed many habitats and species.

Research to promote the vested interests and profits of the corporate world or develop more efficient and powerful ways to kill people is hardly going to be about how to nurture nature and protect life.

Empirical science is a useful tool to observe things and create technologies is blind to other dimensions of life such as the intuitive, instinctive and feeling non-rational realms of experience. Discuss homoeopathy or astrology with a scientist and you might be met with derision. Even when you explain these are languages that speak of energy phenomena rather than empirical observations of the material world, you are likely to encounter scorn.

Yet the numinous is where the sacred and the soul of humanity lies - and we need that soul now more than ever.

'Man has to awaken to wonder - and so perhaps do peoples. Science is a way of sending him to sleep again.' Ludwig Wittgenstein

Would you like a Tarot reading?   Back off - I'm a scientist!

Cultural dynamics within society are another root of this tragedy. We live in an individualised society where laws with penalties controlling what we eat, where we travel, how many children we have etc. look like violations of our 'rights'. And the rights of the individual within the politics of modern capitalism are held to be more significant than the responsibilities of community.

Otherwise we would see clearly that the fact the top 1% own 43% of all personal wealth while the bottom 50% own only 1% is an appalling injustice not an inevitability. (Credit Suisse Global Wealth report, 2020.)

Most people have no idea how much of our lives is controlled by the matrix of power in the hands of the wealthy and privileged. The powerful elites, who own most of the media and other sources of information, dominate society's narrative and conversation because they control most news, social, web and print media. They do not want us to become aware of the endemic injustices that serve their purpose and so use their powers to protect their privilege.

Explore the universe to find yourself or explore yourself to find the universe - or climb ruthlessly to the top.

For example, talk of the 'rights of the individual' within the context of corporate capitalism is a smokescreen. It hides the oppression of people and exploitation of the natural world by the few so they can protect and maintain their privilege and power.

Corruption is so embedded within our political and economic systems people take it for granted and cannot imagine another way to structure society. For example, the dark underbelly of modern politics gives corporate greed free rein via the lobbying industry, campaign contributions and media manipulation - and we have come to think this is inevitable. We have lost sight of how we could organise a society where cooperation and friendship are more important than profit and the accumulation of wealth. Yet the fierce individualism and ruthless business deals needed to accumulate money and power are radically different from an appreciation of the responsibilities and interconnectedness needed to nurture life.

It doesn't matter whether you win or lose - it matters whether I do.

Another factor in our collective lack of response to the eco-emergency is our consumerist version of happiness has addicted us to the material world. What we long for, freedom, justice, truth, fulfilment, safety, adventure, love, happiness... has been sold to us as achievable only through buying things. That way enormous profits can be made out of our natural longing.

As a consequence work is no longer a form of creativity with dignity and meaning, it is alienated labour where we do what we are ordered to by corporations that are purely about profit, whatever their PR propaganda. We chain ourselves to our desks working to sell the things we later buy with the money we made selling them and imagine this is freedom. But owning things is not happiness and consumer choice is not freedom.

The best things in life aren't things.

We are so conditioned to a work culture that alienates us from our natural selves that we have lost sight of how it could be different. We have two weeks holiday year sold to us by the travel and tourist industries adding to its $10 trillion turnover. Then back to work adding to the $52 trillion pure profit made by the oil and gas industry over the last 50 years. That's $2.8 billion a day.

Just for comparison. On a clear night in a dark area away from city lights you can see about 5,000 stars. Life on Earth began about 3.5 billion years ago. And the universe itself is estimated to be 13.7 billion years old. So that's a hell of a lot of money being made from our work that goes into the pockets of shareholders who have done nothing to generate it except look at their bank balance. Though accountants probably do that for them too.

So without any apparent alternative, we continue to destroy life in the pursuit of what we have been persuaded is happiness, even when it is costing us the Earth.

Would you rather own a Van Gogh painting of a starry night or experience directly the full glory of the Milky Way? You can't have both. Anyone who truly experienced the magnificence of the universe at night and let it speak to their soul would sell the painting and use the $100 million, an estimate of what it would fetch at auction, to serve life.

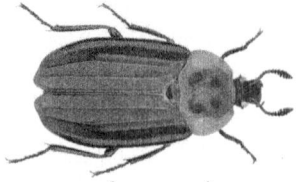

Are you free tonight? No, I'm very expensive.

It is hard for the wealthy to love nature; they have too much they need to guard and protect – or think they do. However well meaning the likes of Bill Gates and Elon Musk believe they are, the very strategies and methodologies that led to their wealth are in opposition to an awareness of the vulnerable interdependencies that lead us to honour, support and respect the natural world.

Though even the very rich will not escape this one. Their underground bunkers or vast ranches in wilderness will not save them from the devastation and collapse of biodiversity and the global microbiome that sustains all life. Whether they know it or not, we are all together in our common humanity this time. Even more deeply we live in the bio-community of all life on this planet.

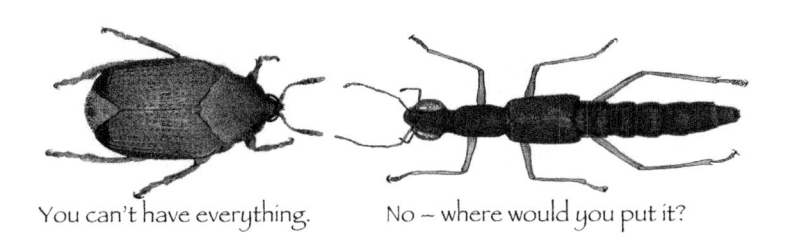

You can't have everything.   No – where would you put it?

'When the last tree is cut, the last river poisoned, and the last fish dead, only then will you discover that you can't eat money.' Cree prophecy.

11   Losing Our Religion

> *Organised religion focuses on a disembodied soul and an after-life that are held to be more important than the living body and life on Earth. This reduces the beautiful animal body to a machine to be used and abused without compassion or concern. It also fosters an arrogant speciesism that has led to an impoverishment of the human spirit and significantly enables our destruction of the natural world.*

Cultural and political dynamics are not the only forces that inhibit our capacity to solve this crisis, our religious and spiritual systems do too. Most religions give the love and life that belong to the animal body to an artificially created idea of a 'soul'. This idea of a human soul, separate from the body, is then considered more important than the living flesh and blood animal body.

The religious focus on a transcendental soul rather than the living spirit of life undermines our respect for nature. It reduces our beautiful animal bodies to machines and turns the living organism into a mechanism to be manipulated at will. It enables us to be cruel to animals and kill them without honouring the sacrifice an animal makes when it gives its life so that we can live. We keep animals incarcerated in sheds with no light or freedom to move. They become so ill they are routinely fed antibiotics before being dragged off in trucks to be slaughtered, often dying en route in pain and panic. We denigrate animal intelligence. We hunt wild creatures, not for food, for sport. We use them in painful experiments. We work them to death. And we do all this without shame because the suffering of animals is of little consequence.

Animal testing is a very bad idea – we get anxious and give all the wrong answers.

We create gods in our own image. Nomadic hunter-gatherers moved with the sun, ate what the earth produced and prayed to mother goddesses to provide for them. The first farmers were more dependent on the local environment and weather and so agrarian societies worshipped wind, rain and fire gods. In herding societies, such as the Hebrew tribe, you find the one God caring for his flock of chosen souls like a shepherd. The Greek development of democracy and cultural academies in cities was reflected in the community of deities on Mount Olympus. In hierarchical societies with slaves and serfs who had to please their masters or die, the gods higher up the food chain have to be appeased with sacrifices. In communities where cooperation is needed to survive, you pray to gods asking for their help. In warlike nations you need warrior gods who will be on your side in a war. We have created gods in our own image in ways that reflect how we relate with nature.

What created us and is greater than us is nature. Yet the natural world that creates and sustains us has been projected skyward and become the might and power of a God in his heaven. The reality is that we are vulnerable to Mother Nature, not a distant Father God in his heaven.

It is the natural world that feeds us, clothes us, gives us the materials we need for life. We can pray to a god all we like but if the crops fail because of drought or the water is poisoned by pollution no amount of prayers to a far off god will help us. We have been praying to the wrong god. The power and the glory that created us is not in the sky, it is here on Earth, in life. The karma of locating what we need in heaven rather than here on Earth is coming home to roost.

'If you know what life is worth, you will look for yours on earth.' Bob Marley

We all have God inside us.

I hope he likes dung – I've just had lunch.

Maybe we have been running from the reality of death and so created consoling fantasies of a heavenly after-life. Perhaps we turned to the patriarchal power of the male gods because the matriarchal power of Mother Nature was too overwhelming. Perhaps to escape our animal natures and create human culture we had to 'rise above' this muddy earth. Yet in the heart of most religions, whatever the god, lies an arrogant speciesism. In the same way religions say our main purpose is to serve whatever is their version of God, other species have no intrinsic worth and exist merely to serve us.

Can someone please explain why Miss Universe is always from Earth?

This leads to animals suffering all over the world from being used for medicine, fashion, scientific experiments, live-food, exotic pets, entertainment in zoos and circuses, and sports such as racing, fighting and hunting. Because only humans matter, only our interests are important, only we have any value.

It is a paradox: The religious idea of a soul led historically to an evolution of human consciousness. It created an appreciation of the significance and worth of each individual. It raised us up out of the primordial soup of collective belonging and into the freedom of our unique individuality. It gave everyone self-worth and meaning. Yet religion then denies that respect and worth to other species.

According to Genesis, we were created in God's image and given dominion over the other species who are *not* in his image. We then imagine we are superior to all other creatures as they apparently do not have souls. This makes us 'special' and disconnects us further from the rest of life.

Such arrogant speciesism is a denial that the animals with whom we share the same planetary home are our kin. This collective betrayal of our animal ancestors is a form of spiritual narcissism, and a both major factor in our wanton destruction of so many animals and their habitats to the point of their extinction. And there is no coming back from this - extinction is forever.

If God created humans in his own image he needs a style consultant for a serious makeover.

12   The Sacred Body

> *The old God is dead. We have become the supreme beings we once worshipped. This has turned us into spiritual narcissists and destroyed any meaning or value to life other than how it serves us. We need to reconnect with the sacred in a new way. The sacred body is not a God in his heaven; it is the body of life.*

We pay a terrible price for our sense of superiority and individual worth. As soon as we identify ourselves primarily as separate and distinct individuals, not as we once did as members of a family or tribe, we discover a new significance and freedom but we also discover death. Death has less sting when our identity is our belonging to the family or tribe because they live on after the individual's death. When our primary identity is our existence as a unique individual, death is the end.

The psychologist Donald Winnicott suggested that when an ancient Semitic tribe wandering in the Sinai desert first began to understand the significance of the individual 'I', this discovery was so threatening they projected it skyward as the supreme God Jahweh, 'I AM'. This God then gradually returned to Earth through individuals willing to face the challenges of freedom and that the price of that freedom is death. The old God has landed. Each one of us now has the existential freedom to say 'I'm worth it'.

I'm thinking of landing on the moon for the 6th time.
          Wow – you've been to the moon!
No, it's the 6th time I've thought about it.

Many of us want the self-worth, self-importance and maybe even the worship that once belonged only to gods, but we rarely want the responsibilities that go with this. Nor do we embrace authentic freedom because this involves taking complete responsibility for our lives and entails hard work. Neither do we face the reality that death is an intrinsic part of life and so we cling to myths of an after-life that is more important than this life.

Dogmatic religious ideology significantly contributes to the destruction humanity wreaks on the natural world because it alienates us from our fellow animals and our own animal nature. But religious belief also causes harm in other ways.

It leads us to fondly imagine that by following society's laws and whatever are the rules of our chosen religion, we will end up in a paradise for eternity. Life then becomes merely a means to this end. Following the rules becomes more important than living, loving, laughing and enjoying each other and life. So we trade our real souls for a disembodied fantasy. The stark truth is most religions are anti-life death-cults that have fostered an appalling impoverishment of the human spirit and significantly enabled our destruction of the natural world.

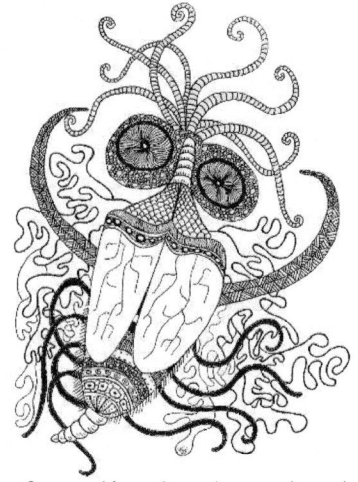

I'm looking for God but don't know where he got lost.

Even though the old God is dead for many of us, we have not lost our religion. We have become the gods we once thought lived in their heaven and now worship ourselves. We are 'worth it' not because of any creativity, work, generosity or action on our part, simply because we exist.

But our being gods means life is no longer sacred, only we are that. The purpose of life then becomes merely to give us what we want. When the meaning of life becomes to fulfil our desires it follows that all other living creatures have no intrinsic significance whatsoever. This give us licence to wantonly use other animals as objects for our own gratification whatever the suffering involved for them.

Each year:

- 72 billion animals are raised and slaughtered worldwide for food, often killed with brutality and dying in agony.
- 1.4 billion cows, water buffalos, sheep, goats, kangaroos and pigs are killed for leather after wretched lives in disgusting conditions in factory farms.
- 50 million foxes, minks, rabbits, lynxes, dogs, beavers, chinchillas and cats are farmed and killed for their fur, often dismembered and skinned while alive because it's cheaper.
- 100 million wild animals are traded illegally internationally.
- 1,000,000 vertebrates are kept imprisoned in zoos.
- 30,000 species, 3 per hour, are being driven to extinction by human activity.
- 35,000 elephants are killed for their ivory, 96 every day.
- 100 million sharks are killed, often merely for their fins for soup.

I'm ill with a really bad case of homo sapiens.

Oh don't worry – it won't last long

The ruthless pursuit of profit by corporate capitalism, the hyper-killing mega-technologies of the industrial-military complex, the global human super-predator, the anti-life propaganda of death phobic religions and the toxic addiction of the human mind to finding 'happiness' through the accumulation of wealth, have formed a deadly matrix of power. This is so destructive it has ruined this beautiful Earth. For most of humanity the natural world now exists merely as a resource for us to use as we want, the lives of other species have no intrinsic value or meaning, and animal suffering is of little consequence. The sacred has vanished.

Some people have told me that when I go on like this, it turns people off. But religion has its tentacles deep into our psyche and is woven into the very fabric of our culture and society to such an extent we no longer notice it. Most people would consider religion either a force for good or an irrelevance, but the deeper truth is that religion has stolen what belongs to nature and falsely laid claim to ownership of the sacred. As a friend Nigel Armistead expressed it, "All religion is rooted in the body - or rather the projection of the 'heaven inside'. Once I know I am part of the natural world and that it's an immense privilege to be alive, the gratitude that flows from this precludes me from ever harming life more than I have to."

How come Judaism, Christianity and Islam have the same God but he keeps telling them different things?

We need to right this spiritual injustice and return the sacred to nature where it belongs. The sacred body is not a God in his heaven; it is the body of life. Here is what matters, not a mythical afterlife. The time will come for us to live our death, then we also will transcend it all. While alive our responsibility lies with life and we need to leave transcendence to the dead. Incarnation not transcendence is what matters now - literally.

Which is why we must live through this eco-crisis with consciousness, creativity, intelligence, compassion and love - because it is about our true human destiny, our rightful place in creation, our future and the future of life on Earth.

'This very Body the Buddha, this very Earth the Lotus Paradise.' Hakuin

We're at a fork in the crossroads on the road to nowhere at a junction with the highway to hell.

Are we there yet?

13   The Beauty of The Beast

> *We have to separate from the instinctual anarchy of our animal-ness in order to live in ordered communities. But to navigate the eco-crisis we need to reconnect with those natural instincts. The energy and awareness that our instinctual connection with life gives us can then take us into a new paradigm of being*

To be human is more than a genetic destiny; we are creatures of culture and society who live in ordered communities with language, abstract thought and self-awareness. The evolution of the human mind and culture, however, has necessitated a distance from the instinctual anarchy of the animal body. To create that distance we have manufactured shame as a force. This shame, together with the fear it engenders, has led us to demean the instincts and intelligence of our animal bodies and the life of other species.

The domination of our own animal-ness by the controlling ego of the world is a primary source of the current eco-crisis. Yet this distance from our animal-ness is an intrinsic aspect of our humanity. It has led to the creation of our culture, our communities, our capacity for thought and language, and the development of philosophy, art and technological prowess. A stark Sophie's Choice: to be living in caves, chewing bones, riddled with lice and fighting off wolves or living in warm homes with the world in the palm of our hands on our phones, facing an eco-apocalypse. It didn't have to be this way – or did it?

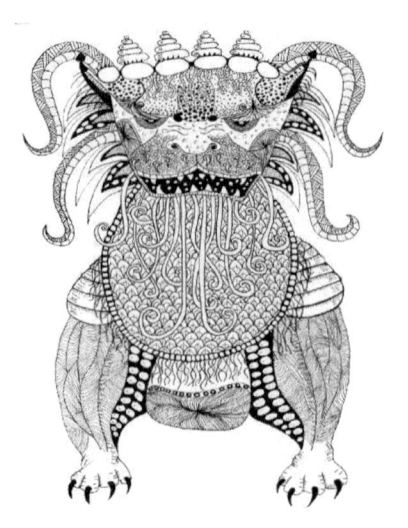

The beauty of the beast is more than skin deep.

Throughout history humans have traded spontaneity for the comforts of civilization and learned to control the natural anarchy of our instincts with laws that inhibit the free expression of our spontaneity, aggression and sexuality. This has enabled us to create complex societies and cultures, to develop language, self-control and abstract thought, to build cities, roads, pyramids and spaceships - but we have paid a great price.

We have cut ourselves off from the instinctual connection to life that informed and nourished our ancestors. We have forgotten we belong to an even greater community, that of all life on Earth. We have lost respect for the animal and in doing so have lost respect for life.

I should be paid to exist - I mean, just look at me!

Rules and ideas of duty and morality, needed for the order of society, can never incorporate the spontaneous anarchic instincts of the animal body, needed to remain alive. This dilemma lies at the core of our human predicament and what is unfolding in the natural world.

In order to arrive at this point in human culture, where our ordered lives are for the most part protected from the challenges of everyday survival, we imprisoned our animal nature in the dungeons of the collective unconscious. However it is now time to release the beast. We need those natural energies, the intelligence of the body and its animal instincts, in order to deal with this crisis in the body of life on Earth.

Many walk away from our instinctive animal-ness into human culture and society, few make the return journey back. It is difficult because to return to our roots as animals requires a release of our anarchic instincts and human culture depends upon their repression and control. How to re-embrace our instincts when our training as children was to dominate and control them? How to incorporate our animal nature when being human is often defined in opposition to being animals?

I used to be someone – but that was Zen, this is Tao.

No other species divides itself against itself. Yet to enter human culture we have to alienate ourselves from our natural energy and divide ourselves against our spontaneous energy. This is in order to analyse our experience, control our instincts, follow rules, learn language and develop principles. For a start no school would have us if we continued to bite friends, grab food and steal toys. Yet the integrity of morality and control is only a partial integrity.

The strategy of divide and rule has given us great power. We have developed the capacity for language, thought and self-awareness, intrinsic aspects of our human nature, but this is only half the story. The journey is not over until we return to our roots – the animal body.

Only when we re-embrace the energies and instincts of the body do we develop a mature integrity, a wholeness that includes our animal nature as part of our human nature. Yet how do we reclaim and re-embrace the instinctual anarchy of the beast without compromising our core principles? We have to listen to our body energy and learn to trust our instincts.

I don't know whether to stop being silly or just be myself.

14   The Politics of Experience.

> *We have to learn to control our spontaneous energy to live in peaceful communities. Yet we are not whole until we re-embrace the instincts and spontaneity we had to abandon. We need this mature integrity so that we do not re-create in our new communities the old order that is based on a rejection and denigration of our own animal-ness.*

We have imprisoned our natural energy in a cage of tension, fear and shame. We need to release ourselves. Which is difficult because to liberate our natural energy involves walking away from the very conditioning that has made us human.

We have to question deeply held beliefs about how we should behave. We have to go beyond old ideas of what is right and wrong. We are likely to be condemned by those with vested interests in maintaining the status quo when they see these wild uncontrolled energies being released. We may be attacked by people afraid of their own natural energy and who feel threatened by our spontaneity and free expression. But unless we re-embrace the energies and life force of the animal we also are, we remain immature, lacking true integrity, and our alienation from the natural world will continue.

Judge me by all means - then remember
to be perfect for the rest of your life.

Controlling the spontaneous expression of our energy is essential. Society would collapse without a collective agreement to drive on the left, pay for food and bite back our rage in traffic. The difficulty is in the way we teach children to conform and control themselves. We make them afraid of the consequences of being 'naughty' and feel ashamed of themselves when they do something 'wrong'. As a result we have all internalised, to differing degrees, fear and shame in relation to our natural energy. The aboriginals of Australia have a better way. When a child does something 'wrong', their shadow is reprimanded. The child too tells their shadow off – 'naughty shadow, you made me do it, you must stop it!' The child internalises the learning but not the shame.

I stopped fighting my inner demons and went over to their side.

The conditioned fear and existential shame, present in us all to differing degrees, corrodes our beings. Over time we end up dominating other forms of life in the same way we do our own life energy. Such controlling and controlled behaviour can appear on the surface to be a form of principled morality and considered dutiful, reliable, steady. The deeper reality is very different.

The domination of our animal needs and instincts by our will enables us to make money, climb the corporate ladder or have a career in politics, but we lose vital aspects of our humanity. To be always and everywhere in control of our energy keeps us confined within our fears, though the fear is mostly unconscious. Our unacknowledged fear and shame then undermine our natural energy further.

We lose our spontaneity. We dominate life in a kind of bullying we think is normal. We become numb to the feelings and sensations in our bodies and rely instead on our intellect to guide us. We cut ourselves off from our vulnerability and lose our compassion. We are driven to seek power, money, fame, or whatever we want, regardless of the cost to others. We lose our capacity to love. And we have no idea that what is motivating us is fear of life and shame of our natural selves. Nor do we have any understanding of what we have lost.

You should be ashamed of yourself! | Why?

You might think I'm exaggerating the extent of unhappiness in our culture and society, but much of the unhappiness people feel in our modern culture lives in the body. It is not expressed or experienced directly and is buried in the unconscious body. Much chronic systemic disease is a profound unhappiness that has been metabolised into illness. And the statistics of chronic ill health are truly shocking.

51.8% of people in the US are chronically ill with diseases for which there is no cure and which are managed with drugs. In Germany, 50% of people report living with chronic conditions that require medication and affect their capacity to operate in life. The average age of women in the UK diagnosed with long-term illness significantly affecting their quality of life is 44y.

There is little social context to talk about how deeply we are alienated from and deprived of our natural selves and how much this hurts us. So we turn to the language of illness with no idea how miserable we are. Conversations about migraines, chronic fatigue, hip and knee replacements, on-going medical conditions etc. are often as much about how sad, lonely, angry and afraid many people are. And so we distract ourselves from our true selves in a consumer paradise of TV entertainment, exotic holidays, ready-made meals delivered to our door, while we binge watch Netflix and connect with each other by social media. This, we have been told again and again by ads, the corporate world and the political and wealthy elite, is 'the good life'. And we have come to believe it. It may be OK but it is not that good.

Here's a get better soon card.

But I'm not ill.

No, but I think you can get better.

The reality of our unhappy alienation from our natural freedom as animals will erupt when the eco-apocalypse impacts us even more deeply than it has already. When the food distribution network fails and we have to grow our own food, oil is rationed and prohibitively expensive, energy supplies are compromised and we are cold, hungry, and in the dark with no phone, no shopping, no phone or TV, the unhappy animal will emerge. And it will be, if not depressed and despairing, fighting, enraged and violent.

Allegedly 1 out of 4 are mentally unbalanced.
So if 3 of your close friends seem Ok then...

We live in a deep, and mostly unconscious, fear of life. The corrosion of our souls through fear of ourselves, of each other and of life itself, is a hidden source of the eco-apocalypse we have unleashed on the natural world. We think the good life is to live in grand houses wearing Rolex watches and diamonds, with Lamborghinis on the drive and flying in private jets to exotic places all over the world, even when it means we are turning those places into deserts. We are too afraid to come to life, because to be alive is to be vulnerable, able to be wounded, to be spontaneous and sometimes out of control. We pursue power over life because we're too afraid of raw experience. We destroy Earth to create the 'good' life. We annihilate life in order to get what we want. There has to be another way.

15   Divide and Rule

> *Humanity values the intellectual mind more than the animal body. But without the body we are nothing. Any species that neglects its animal body soon becomes extinct. Yet our human alienation from the life in our bodies creates self-awareness. One of humanity's great creative journeys is a transmutation of pure existence into a conscious awareness of existence. Through our loss and rediscovery of life the universe creates a consciousness of itself.*

The most fantastic construction of the human mind has been the creation of the world. Out of the anarchic flow of instinctual energy that runs through our animal bodies and makes us breathe, run, play, make love, fight, and laugh, we have created societies of amazing complexity with machines and technologies that have given us the myriad wonders of the world. However, the continuation of the current world is costing us our lives. We need to decide – do we want the world or do we want life?

Other animals do not have this conflict. They live in a surrender to life in which impulse and action are one. Nothing interferes with their simple authenticity and spontaneity. This is the paradise of pure being the other animals never left. We exiled ourselves from this Garden of Eden when we divided life into good and evil and split life and ourselves in two. This capacity to divide and rule gave us great power over life. But the price was an abandonment of our natural integrity. As a consequence we live in perpetual conflict with our natural selves and have a bereavement that leaves us forever longing for a paradise lost.

For the real knowledge of good and evil, forget the apple - eat the snake.

The greatest gift and greatest curse of our species has been this collective betrayal of the animal body. Yet we can be human only to the degree we can be animal. We can be alive only so long as we care for the animal body. Any species that neglects its animal body soon becomes extinct. Which is the void we are staring into, a dark flight down into the hyper-oblivion that is the ultimate death – extinction.

To choose life and create a different future from the catastrophic death-void facing us, the materialist conditioning of the world-ego with its addiction to power must give way to the instinctual intelligence of the body. We must disentangle from the world with its deadly desires and ruthless greed, detoxify ourselves from the hyper-materialist conditioning of the global politico-economic matrix, cease our lethal super-hunting and overuse of the Earth's resources, and the human world-ego must give up its addiction to power and surrender to the demands of life.

The necessary radical transformation of the socio-political matrix of our modern world, together with its manifestation within the ego of each one of us, will not be easy. The animal body is intrinsically vulnerable; it hurts, bleeds and dies. We have evolved the world with its mighty technological prowess in part to protect that vulnerability. We live inside the protected shell of the world-machine like the 'soft green blob' inside a Dalek. As a result we are deeply entangled with the world and any radical change will elicit primal fears. The journey back into our animal-ness is a kind of death. The ego of the world in each of us has to die.

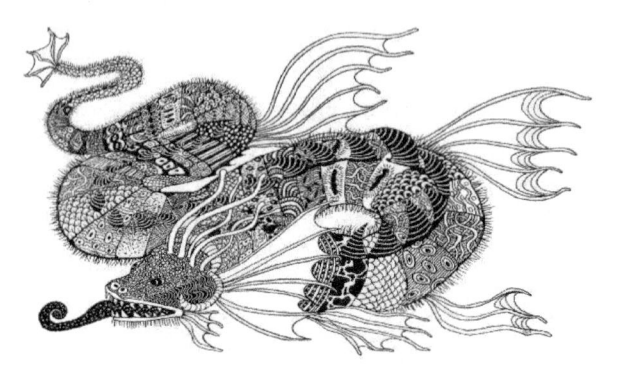

Find what you love – then let it kill you.

A Zen story tells of a fish in the ocean who swims in blissful ignorance of the sea all around her. One day she is washed up onto the shore. She struggles in agony to breathe until another wave washes her back into the ocean. Now she is aware of the sea all around her. We are that fish. Our destiny seems to involve first separating from the spontaneous uninhibited flow of our life energy, becoming therefore consciously aware of life, and then returning to life with this knowledge to serve life.

Other species of animals do not have a conditioned cultural ego. They simply *are* alive; they do not *know* they are alive. It is a great responsibility and a crucial part of our human meaning and fulfilment to bring the gift of our conscious awareness of life, created through our very alienation from life, back to the living body of life on Earth. This return to our roots, together with the powers and knowledge we acquired through separating from them, is a sacred quest.

One of the great human journeys of life is the alchemical transmutation of pure existence into a conscious awareness of existence. Though this has significance and meaning beyond the destiny of our own species. Through our loss and rediscovery of life, the universe creates a consciousness of itself.

The universe is a figment of its own imagination.

The body of the cosmos, the body of life and the animal body of humanity are all connected in the complex mystery of existence. That we have neglected these dimensions of our humanity and instead focused almost exclusively on the material aspects of life is our tragedy - which has now become a tragedy for all life on Earth. We need to re-embrace the numinous wisdom of the body. Even though what unfolds at a cosmic level is ultimately a mystery beyond our comprehension, we are playing our part in a vast drama within which existence becomes reality, reality comes to life, life becomes conscious, consciousness becomes love, and outside the dimensions of space and time this love is possibly what called existence into being in the first place. Why else would all this be happening if not for love?

'Love is a sacred energy. It is the blood of all evolution.' Teilhard de Chardin

The most intimate piece of Earth, and the one for which we are completely responsible, is our own animal body. This body is more than we conceive, believe or think it is. Until we learn its secret wisdom we will continue to use and abuse the body of life on Earth out of ignorance, fear and greed. Let us therefore explore the animal-body and let its ancient visceral instinctual wisdom speak to us of things we desperately need to hear.

This body is a gift from God.

I hope you kept the receipt - you might want to exchange those horns for feelers or wings or something.

16   The Unconscious Is The Body

> *Our human mind thinks of reality in terms of separate objects but life is a flow of energy. Even our bodies are not as we believe, objects that belong to us. The animal body and its instincts are part of the great river of life. The body is the unconscious, a vast untapped resource. We need to tap into the wisdom of the body to help us navigate what is to come.*

We perceive the world through our senses. The information comes into us in the form of energy, such as wavelengths of light or the vibration of sound waves, our bodies and brains then interpret these as sights, sounds, smells etc. We construct the world 'out there' from within our bodies through neurological, metabolic, cellular activity of various kinds. Perception of reality is not therefore a passive experience; it is a creative operation that involves actively constructing a map of reality. We might interpret a set of light waves and sound vibrations as a tree, a fox may perceive a hiding place, a beetle, a leaf-fest, a fungus, a node in a bio-web of information exchange and so on. We perform the same active creative perception in relation to ourselves. The body for example is more than we think it is.

I know a joke about perception but you might not laugh – it depends how you look at it.

We think of the body as an object, but the body is not a thing; it is a constant flow of energy. The body is life. And life is a constant flow. Out of the river of life, our human mind creates a world of separate objects, each with its own existence in time and space. This division of the energy flow of life into discrete objects allows us to know ourselves as separate and unique individuals but this objectified universe is only one reality. Another is that the universe is pure energy, one body with multiple forms that continually change.

Out of the flow of energy that is the life of the body we construct with our minds the idea of an object that is 'me', an objectified body that is 'mine'. This self-objectification gives us power, freedom and autonomy - yet also loneliness, anxiety and death. Loneliness, because there is only one unique 'I' in the whole universe. Anxiety, because in a world where 'eat or be eaten' is the law of the jungle, everything other than 'me' is a potential threat. Death, because the 'I' that is me dies and is gone forever.

If I weren't me I'd like to be you.   If I weren't me I'd like to be me too.

Other animals, remaining at one with the undifferentiated flow of life, do not suffer this anguish. Their innocent instinctual beingness is the paradise from which we have been exiled in order to know ourselves.

Eventually our division of energy into things, union into separateness, spontaneity into thought, and the endless moment into chronological time become what we believe is reality. We forget there is another way of being. The body, however, does not forget. Everything that has ever happened to us has left its trace in some form or other in our bodies, in the tidal ebb and flow of our hormones, in our electric current of our neural networks, in the metronomic beat of our hearts, in the kinaesthetic memory of our muscles, in the continual metabolic homeostasis operating day and night to keep us alive. Our bodies hold a map of our history and our experience. The unconscious is not an abstract idea invented by Freud, it is the living breathing reality of the body.

When we talk about a feeling, motivation, desire or conflict being unconscious, we mean it lives in our body, in our energy, but not in our conscious minds. The journey into the body therefore takes us into a direct experience of our unconscious process. We discover parts of us that exist beyond our identification with our personality and our separate ego-self. We connect with our energy, not only our thoughts. We enter the feeling instincts of the body, which reveal we are more than we ever imagined. We go beyond our belief that we are solely separate unique individuals and discover we are part of an amazing mystery beyond our comprehension.

We come to life and discover, our glorious instinctual heritage is not lost, it lives on in the unconscious energy of our bodies.

Don't believe everything you think.

Human life is complex. To become human is to enter a labyrinth of contradictions and conflicts. Self and other. Power and vulnerability. Chaos and order. Thought and feeling. Freedom and responsibility. Sanity and madness. Clarity and confusion. Belonging and aloneness. The list of conflicting polar opposite energies within the human psyche is as long as human history.

There are no simple resolutions to these continual conflicts. If there were, we'd learn the million rules of how to live life alongside the times tables in school. There are no rules; we have to find our own way through the labyrinth. The conflict and tension between these opposing polarities of experience and behaviour force us to be spontaneous, creative and respond afresh in each moment. In other words to be alive.

Following the rules and doing it 'right' is not how we come to life. We have to learn certain rules and how to control ourselves when we are young. Then in our maturity we become free to make a conscious decision whether to abide by them or do it our own way. The dialectics of freedom: first we are in an instinctive flow like all animals (thesis), then we learn to control this flow of energy with our intellectual minds (antithesis), then we discover the freedom to follow our instincts or our intellect according to the situation (synthesis). Freedom lies in the synthesis.

I'm a philosopher and think about the existential dialectics of beetlehood and stuff.

I'm a one too but can't think what to think about.

Whatever the community-ark we create to carry us through the eco-crisis we need to organise within it time and space for our natural energy and animal instincts to run spontaneously and freely. If we don't, we'll end up with the same alienation from first of all our own life force and then from life itself that has been a major source of this eco-catastrophe in the first place.

We will explore this in later chapters. First let us look at how the human ego itself is based on fear. Because we need to release that fear in order to navigate the future with a love of life right in the heart of our endeavours. There is no other way.

17   Maps of Fear

> *As children, we learn to control our experience and behaviour through tension in our bodies. These patterns of tension become habitual and form part of our sense of self. To connect with the rich living energy of our bodies and the free flowing life force of our animal-ness we need to relax this control and face the fears that will be released. This will liberate us from the rules of behaviour and control that have kept us restricted since childhood and reconnect us with our natural spontaneity.*

We control the way life and feeling flow through our body as a way to control our experience and behaviour. As children, we learn to tense our muscles and restrict our breathing in an attempt to protect us from what we fear happening, to numb feelings that would otherwise overwhelm us, and to stop spontaneous actions that we have learned cause trouble. Eventually these patterns of tension in our bodies become ingrained and habitual. Hunched shoulders, inhibited breathing, tense necks, tight mouths, restricted movement, low energy, slow reflexes and so on are all manifestations of our attempts to manoeuvre through life with minimum stress and pain.

It's been proved, reality is the prime cause of stress.

Over time we become habituated to our fear and no longer notice the resulting tension in our bodies. We cease to be aware how afraid we are, how much control we have placed on ourselves, and how much our behaviour is driven by those unconscious fears. To move beyond the cultural ego of the world and reconnect with the living energy of our animal body, we have to relax this habitual and unconscious control. But like 'be happy' and 'don't worry' or 'just relax', this is far easier said than done.

Letting go of these deep tension involves facing all our fears that led to the tension and control in the first place. This, of course, is a frightening and uncomfortable experience. And why few make the return journey back into our roots, the body, and why most of us remain energetically alienated from our animal nature the whole of our lives.

The human ego, the 'me' I think I am, is not the true energy of our life force. It is a construction we imposed on ourselves to protect us from experiences and behaviours that threaten us. For each of us this has created a particular personality that we think is who and what we are. Yet this sense of self, our ego, our personality, is something we have constructed to help us navigate life and not who we truly are.

The energy of our real self and our natural life force is more complex, expansive, rich and alive than any ego identity we think is who we are. Who we truly are has both more animal-ness and more humanity than any ego self.

I must be God - because when I pray I find I'm talking to myself.

The conscious ego is the psychic counterpart of the tension in our bodies. Mentally and psychologically the ego is the set of expectations and habits of behaviour and thought we call our personality. Physically and physiologically the ego consists of the habitual tensions in our bodies we maintain to control our feelings and spontaneous movements. The source of the ego is our fear of ourselves and life. The tension in the muscles of our body is therefore a map of our fear.

Much of that fear is unconscious but controls our behaviour all the same. In the same way our bodies find it hard to let go of the deep tension in our muscles because we are afraid of the feelings that will flood us, the ego self is afraid of being spontaneous because our natural life force is anarchic, unpredictable and outside our conscious control. To reconnect with the full aliveness of our animal bodies however involves releasing this deep tension and as a consequence re-experiencing our deepest fears.

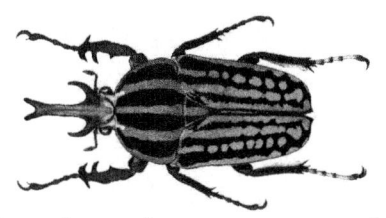

I tried yoga but prefer stress – it's not as boring.

When the tension of our ego-control releases, we experience everything we've tried to keep at bay. Rage, need, vulnerability, anxiety, sadness, aggression, sexuality, helplessness... whatever we are most afraid of within ourselves, our most intimate fears, the energies we had to bury as children, these return as living experiences in our bodies. We might scream, shout and make loud noises. Our bodies might make unusual uncontrolled movements. We might shake, beat cushions or run around naked. We might dance in moonlight, sing nonsensical songs, or sit completely still and silent. This is why when we first connect with our natural energy, we need a safe context either alone or with others who understand what is happening. The protection of a safe place allows our body to unfold itself freely without the fear of disapproval, condemnation or interference that would otherwise inhibit us.

I don't suffer from insanity, I enjoy it.

We may believe it is a sign of immaturity to be angry, wrong to covet our neighbour's ox, Tesla car or new conservatory, immoral to feel sexually attracted to a stranger, dissolute and depraved to drink and take drugs, and so on. But these are natural energies of human animals trying to make good lives for themselves. It is what we do with these urges and feelings that matters, not whether we have them or not.

The First Law of Thermodynamics is that energy can neither be created nor destroyed, only transformed. If we repress our life force, those energies do not simply disappear. In the darkness of the unconscious they devolve into more malevolent distortions of our humanity. If we never feel our anger, we are likely to become righteous moralists. If we never allow our sexuality, we tend to condemn the pleasures of others. If we deny completely our capacity to kill, we will shut down life in a more insidious way while imagining we are being sensitive and compassionate. How we relate with the energies of life directly reflects how we relate with our own life energy. We cannot escape ourselves.

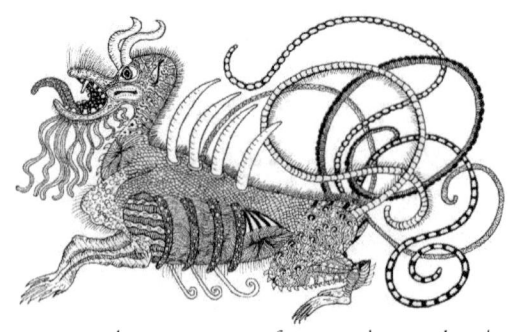

Help! I keep meeting what I'm running from on the road I take to avoid it.

18 The Crazy Wisdom

> *When we control our spontaneity and self-expression to conform to the demands of society, those impulses do not disappear, they become locked inside our bodies. We then dominate and control life around us in the same way we dominate and control our own life energy. Relaxing this control leads to a healthier relationship with first the life flowing through our own bodies and then life itself.*

In the east there are said to be three paths through life. The Hinayana path, where you follow established rules and the guidance of an enlightened master, the Mahayana path, where you give your life in service to the greater community, and the Vajrayana or Tantric path, where you leave all paths to follow a 'crazy wisdom' and 'dance in the fields'.

I'm the Dalai Beetle -
Can I help you?

Yeah, what's the meaning of life?
But make it quick - I've an important meeting in half an hour.

In the middle of a lake in Tibet is a temple built by the 6th Dalai Lama in C14th. The ground floor is a Hinayana temple built in the Chinese style. On feast days the local community would be invited to visit for food and meditation. The next floor is a Mahayana temple built in the Tibetan style. Only the monks who had taken their Bodhisattva vows were permitted to enter here. The top temple is the Tantric temple and built in the Mongol style. Only the Dalia Lama and a small group of chosen disciples could enter here.

The Tantric temple is a single room reached through a trapdoor. It is decorated with paintings that are completely different from the thangkas of the lower temples. Alongside images of deities and Buddhas are pictures of childbirth, violence, menstruation, making love, eyeballs being gouged out, hunting, stabbings, ecstatic dance, eating meat, getting drunk and stoned and so on. The 6th Dalai Lama took his chosen few into this temple where they drank alcohol, ate meat, fought, danced, invited women with them, smoked dope, made love and broke every one of their Bodhisattva vows. They behaved in ways that appeared exactly like the raucous anarchy in local taverns. Chogyam Trungpa said that when the Bodhisattvas in the middle temple heard what was going on above them, they were utterly shocked. Yet this was the Dalai Lama. It was so incongruent they all fell down in a faint.

When I hear what religious people get up to,
I thank God for making me an atheist.

Yet what was happening in the top Tantric temple was not like a drunken revel in a local tavern. Each monk had gone through a thorough training in the Bodhisattva tradition where you place your whole life in the service of all sentient beings. They had surrendered so completely to this discipline it had become part of their being. So when they let-go into their instinctual energy this was not an anarchic free-for-all, it was true freedom. Having completely detached from their ego desires they could allow the energy of the instincts free rein and not be driven by them. The life force of their bodies was given free expression within the context of their conscious awareness.

An interviewer asked Tenzing Norgay and Edmund Hillary, the first men to reach the top of Chomolungma, Mount Everest, why they did it. They replied, 'Because it exists.' Some people somewhere have to experience our human darkness and animalness with consciousness and love - because they exist.

These mountains are hill-areas.

I'm not laughing, I'm out of breath. It all looked a lot flatter on the map.

The life of the animal body and its instincts are outside the cultural constraints, beliefs, religious dogmas, social mores, moral codes, principled behaviour that we think should always guide our actions. But these energies and impulses are real and reality is a greater force than our minds can comprehend. What *is* happening is more significant than what I want, think or believe *should be* happening. These instinctual impulses, energies and urges therefore have meaning, whatever we think of them, because they are real. To always and everywhere be in control of these energies and prevent them expression causes harm to the beautiful vulnerable animal body.

Yet we need to act with principled morality else there would be no community, social structures or culture of any kind. We would be living with no order or laws in an anarchy of raw instinct. Children have to learn to 'behave' else they would be thrown out of every classroom, school play and birthday party they attended. The animal body therefore has to suffer in order for us to enter human society and become human. We have gained the whole world but suffer the loss of our life force.

Life's already yours so why try to conquer it?

In the 1970s I went to India and became a disciple of a Tantric guru now known as Osho. I had no idea what I was letting myself in for. Everything happened. What unfolded was the brightest enlightenment of love and freedom through to dark enactments of ruthless abuse of power. Some saw only the light, others only the dark. Some of us saw both sides of a journey that embraced the full spectrum of our humanity. We found we had been initiated into the top temple where everything happens, even our human darkness, within the context of a conscious love of life.

But none of us was a Dalai Lama and we were condemned on all sides. The devoted followers were outraged when we spoke of the dark side of that story. Straight society judged us as immoral and self-indulgent. Intellectuals sneered when we spoke of the intelligence of the instincts and the wisdom of the body. The psycho-spiritual well-ness brigade told us we were negative and must raise our vibrational level. And when we began to speak of the eco-catastrophe heading our way, very few listened to what we had to say about the psycho-spiritual undercurrents to this crisis and its roots in a collective betrayal of the animal body. But you cannot magically create a utopia through yoga, organic food, scented candles, meditation and aromatherapy. Of course enjoy them while you can if you want to, but they won't save you from the eco-apocalypse.

Why are you chucking those yoga mats and scented candles in the bin?

I've been chillin' with prada-hippies drinking green tea, sniffing incense & shit for weeks and still I wanna punch people!

The mind is a useful tool for manipulating reality, but not for experiencing it. Our bodies experience life directly. The eco-crisis is a crisis in the body of life itself; therefore the guidance we need is not only in the intellectual understanding of our minds, it is to be found also in the wisdom of the instincts in our bodies. For this we need to dis-identify from our minds and enter the world of energy. This world follows different laws.

When we tune in on the subtle energies and sensations of our bodies, breathe deeply and feel, listen to the instinctual language of animals, communicate with the spirits of soul-healing plants such as Ayahuasca and mushrooms, dance with complete freedom for our bodies to move how they wish, or whatever is our way, we make discoveries of a different kind. We are no longer confined to understanding merely what can be analysed and defined. We begin to comprehend the deeper dynamics of life that lie beyond the frontiers of the mind. And we bring a deeper intelligence and understanding to bear on the eco-catastrophe.

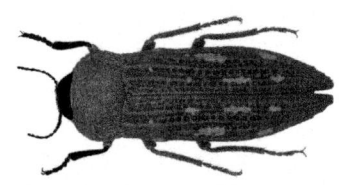

Reality's OK I guess, but I wouldn't want to live there.

19 Search For the Wilderness Inside Yourself

> *We have to control our natural energy, otherwise society would become a dangerous anarchy. But to be always and everywhere in control of our energy leads to an unhappy alienation from life. We need safe places where our bodies can move and express themselves in complete freedom otherwise we lose our vital life-force. Which we need to navigate the future.*

The animal body suffers when it has to live within the rules of human culture and society. Yet without self-control and principled morality there would be no order or social structures to organise and protect us, just an anarchic unfolding of raw energy. Living in communities is essential for our humanity. But though we gain the world but lose aspects of our life force. Watch a tiger wrestle with a boar, a gannet dive for fish in the sea, a chimpanzee race through the forest or a group of orcas take down a humpback calf. That same totality belongs to us. We need to get it back. That is if we are to have any chance of surviving the eco-apocalypse.

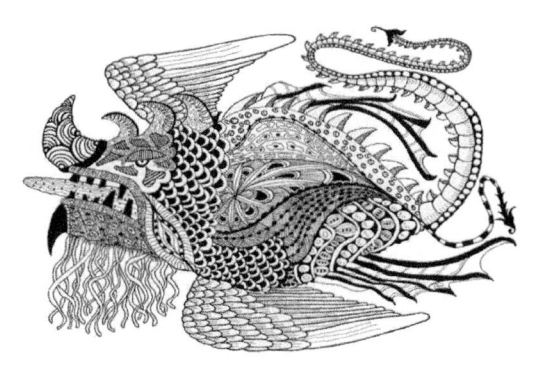

When I'm good I'm very good, but when I'm bad I'm even better.

To protect our communities, we interfere with the flow of energy through our bodies continually. With the best of intentions, we try to become aware of our anger and not inflict it on another. We do our best to explore conflict rather than go to war. We (mostly) repress sexual desire for a friend's partner, bite back jealousy for a colleague's success, stop ourselves stealing from shops and so on. All of which protects us from certain harms but hurts our animal energy in other ways. We harm life in trying not to cause harm.

If a sheepdog always and everywhere has to do what the farmer orders and is never allowed to run free in a pack, bark at birds, chase squirrels, play with other dogs, they will die young and unhappy. We do something similar to our bodies. We do not die young because our medical technologies and pharmaceutical drugs keep us going but most people in industrialised societies are unhappy, chronically sick and only partially alive. Often without knowing it because they do not know what they are missing.

I have an inferiority complex but it's not a very good one.

Our body energy needs at least occasionally to flow with no restraint, control, suppression or interference from our more conscious selves - otherwise we lose much more than we know. In modern culture we no longer talk with plants or have conversations with the birds. We do not commune and play with animals other than our pets. We do not listen while rocks tell us their stories or swim with octopuses as friends. We have lost so much that most people think these kinds of experiences are crazy or just poetic licence. But they are real. Though they are not of the intellectual mind; they are experiences and sensations of the human animal body.

I'm not crazy but the voices in my head might be.

Humanity has not resolved the conflict between free expression and self-control and so we must each resolve for ourselves the conflicting energies of order and chaos, will and spontaneity, tension and relaxation, sharing and withholding, acting out and self reflection, and so on. Yet without this continual challenge to find our own way through the labyrinth of our humanity, we would be merely carbon copies of each other. At the same time these conflicts have driven us into the eco-crisis of the Anthropocene Extinction.

Unlike other animals, we are consciously aware of life and therefore know how good it is to be alive. With that knowledge also comes the understanding that one day our life will end and we will die. To try and avoid this fateful inevitability we sacrifice the goodness of life for safety. The glorious instinctual delight and happiness of the natural body in simply being alive is our birth right yet the politics of experience demands we forsake this in order to have power over life to keep us safe. But the most dangerous path of all is to seek safety at all costs. Having power over life then becomes more important than experiencing life. We sacrifice life to stay alive. To stay sane, we drive ourselves crazy. To keep safe we kill life.

Safety first. Just kidding. Dung and rotting compost first. Safety is like maybe tenth or something.

Continual control over our natural energy by our ideas of what is right and wrong, our principled commitment to doing no harm, our conviction that this control is the 'right' way to behave, mean our culturally created minds dominate our animal selves. In modern culture the mind almost completely dominates the body. Our bodies are rarely if ever allowed to run free. Yet without there being a place and time somewhere for the total liberation of our animal energies we lose the potency of our aliveness. And we need to be as fully alive as possible to deal with what is coming.

We need protected and safe places for our animal bodies to run free from restraint and interference. This is partly because many people are afraid when they see the instincts being allowed free expression. They are threatened at this lack of control and tend to condemn and judge what they do not understand. Yet no one can truly understand, 'stand under', the life of the body - because the body is what stands under each of us. And only the body of life stands under us all.

I went out of my mind and have no plans to go back.

The eco-Apocalypse is a crisis in the body of life. The body of our life, therefore, holds the answers. The journey into the body takes us through our fears and liberates not only our personal energy, it releases the instinctive energies of humanity that have been incarcerated in the collective unconscious for millennia. Once released, these living energies and their natural wisdom will help us navigate the geo-bio-catastrophe upon us.

Wherever you meet to plan your future, in forests, on beaches, on the streets or in living rooms, parks or cafés, you will need to explore many dimensions of our humanity. If you are exploring the possibility of living in a community then discussions on the practical aspects of building a community, growing food, creating homes, ensuring warmth, shelter and water are available, and finding ways to organise the basic needs for survival will be needed. Explore what might be the rules of the community and how you make decisions, how you care for children and what to teach them. Discover what you need in terms of communal areas, private spaces and how to balance togetherness and aloneness, order and spontaneity, freedom and commitment, self and other. Also plan how you will take care of the invisible psycho-spiritual dimensions of human life.

The instinctive energies of humanity have been neglected in modern culture to our tragic cost. There is no point recreating in new communities the same dynamics that have led to this crisis. We need times when, like the Tibetan Tantrikas in their top temple, we allow our life energy to flow in absolute freedom. It is time to release the beast.

Which would you rather be – Satan or nothing?

I think I'll take the lesser of two weevils thank you.

20   Releasing the Beast

> *When we tune into the sensations and experiences of the body, we liberate not only our personal energy, we release energies that have been incarcerated in the collective unconscious for millennia. Once released, these living energies and their instinctual wisdom will help us navigate the geo-bio catastrophe upon us.*

When we explore the world of energy we discover new freedoms, our life force returns and our bodies are liberated from cultural, religious, ideological, sociological and psychological constraints that have been controlling us. We feel more alive and spontaneous with less fear and shame. We also become aware of how much harm we've done, first to our own bodies and then to life itself. We begin to realise that doing only what we think is 'right' is deeply 'wrong'. It has kept us caged. The politics of human experience entraps the animal body in a prison of unconscious tension.

I used to be normal but it drove me insane.

The one animal we are completely responsible for, the one piece of Earth for which we are solely accountable, is our own body. Yet the personal is political. The politics of experience that plays out within our own body can be as destructive and harmful as the power dynamics at work collectively and globally. Just as we need to liberate life from humanity's greed and abuse, we need to liberate ourselves from ourselves. If only because what we do to ourselves we will do to life - because we are life.

'The human body is the most vulnerable, the only source of all joy, all suffering and all truth.' Alina Szapocznikow, sculptor and Holocaust survivor.

Our bodies are 90% water.

So basically we're melons with existential anxiety.

To help free your animal-bodies from the mind-control of your conditioning, here are a few suggestions:

Shake, run, skip, crawl, swim, stamp, roll, climb, jump, stretch, wriggle, tremble, bounce.
Shout, scream, laugh, cry and talk gibberish.
Lie on the ground and let insects crawl over you.
Climb mountains, swim in rivers, wander off the beaten path.
Breathe deeply, jump into a cold lake and swim.

Surf waves, scuba dive, camp in wilderness.
Walk a mile in slow motion.
Feel your anger, rage and hatred, your compassion, empathy and kindness, your resentment, jealousy and aggression, your sadness, heartbreak and remorse.
Lie in long grass, smell the air and listen to the summer.
Beat cushions, stamp on carpets, scream at the sky.
Walk through fields with no idea where you are headed.
Look into the eyes of both friends and enemies.
Let the soul medicines of Ayahuasca, Iboga, Peyote, mushrooms speak to you.
Howl with the wind, laugh with stars, speak with plants and talk with rocks.
Sit in a cave and stare into darkness.
Go into the night raging like a jaguar, rampaging like an elephant, howling like a wolf.
Go into the night as silent as a bat, as swift as a falcon, as patient as a snake.

We need to exercise our bodies and our minds.

I agree - that's why I think a lot about jogging.

When we first encounter the non-rational instinctual realms of energy, we might think we are going mad. This is because it becomes apparent that the cognitive constructs we have believed are reality reflect merely one dimension of a multi-dimensional universe. The foundations of our belief systems, our cognitive maps of the material world, the intellectual understandings that we think make sense of life are challenged at root. Most intimately, our understanding of ourselves shifts. We discover we are not what we thought we were. Even our body is revealed as more than we imagined. This is profoundly liberating and also deeply disorienting.

Sometimes we need help to reach these other realms of experience though psychotropic plants such as psilocybin mushrooms, peyote, salvia, ayahuasca, marijuana, iboga and coca. Taking mind-altering substances for spiritual awakenings is one of the human universals compiled by Donald Brown that have been found in every culture, all over the world, and throughout history. Of course every medicine with the power to heal also has the power to harm - it would have no potency otherwise. Unfortunately the war on drugs, which is really a war on consciousness, has driven this vital part of our humanity underground.

I've just been on trip advisor but couldn't find anything about Ayahuasca or magic mushrooms.

However, operating underground has kept such plants safe from the pharmaceutical industry and the corporate world. Tobacco was once a friend of humanity used by shamans, the tabaqueros, to enable the speaking of truths and bring peace to conflict. Its shamanic potency has now been lost in the global abuse of this wonderful plant for profit. Fortunately most psychotropic plants continue to work with us synergistically and should we need them, these soul medicines will find us. Plants, like the animals of the Earth, are longing for us to realise our true destiny and will do all they can to help us.

21 Instinctual Love

> *One source of the eco-crisis is that we do not love life enough. Our own individual survival has become more important than anything else in the world. This means we will sacrifice all that makes life worth living to live a little longer in a life that is not therefore worth living. Our collective phobic fear of death has led us to kill life on Earth.*

When we enter the non-rational experience of the animal-body we begin to sense and feel dimensions of life previously unavailable to us. We experience life beyond the frontiers of our ego, in the realm of the numinous and mysterious. We discover life is more important to us than all the money and power in the world. We become aware of the privilege of simply being alive. And it becomes apparent, even though we may not have realised this fully before, how deeply we love life.

Our love of life is so profound it is unafraid of even death.

Life's amazing. You're born crying, life's hard, you die, worms eat you, you're reincarnated as a cockroach and it all happens in the right order!

In the world of energy, the body we think is 'mine' and 'me' is the collection of fearful tension that is our ego - and this body dies. Our animal body however is a body of subtle sensitivity and feeling, the body electric, a flow of energy, and this energy-body cannot die, it can only be transformed.

Our visceral instinctive love of life shows us that death is not as we thought, annihilation; it is the transformation of one form of life into another. Our death is the gift of ourselves back to life as we leave and in this way life is enriched by our life and death.

But we have become identified with our patterns of control over our energy and think our personality is who we are. Here lies the difficulty. On death the body surrenders completely to the processes of life, which, of course, includes death. And on death there is no more tension or control of any kind. The ego dissolves. The personality disappears. The 'me' we think is who we are, is gone.

Why is there's a highway to hell but only a stairway to heaven?

Which do you think carries the most traffic?

The only way to avoid death is not to come alive in the first place. This seems to be the path we have collectively taken. We are so afraid of death we have become morbidly afraid of it and created a death-phobic culture where we deaden ourselves to avoid death, we sacrifice life to remain half-alive, and we stop ourselves feeling in order to survive. One of the roots underlying our destruction of the natural world is the toxic death-phobic nature of human culture and society.

We are naturally afraid of death, it is a form of self-protection, but we must stop sacrificing what makes life precious and meaningful in order to survive a little longer in a life that has therefore lost vitality and meaning. Releasing our instinctual love of life will release us from this half-dead life and back into our full aliveness. We feel all the sensation in our bodies despite that this inevitably means alongside joy, laughter and love we experience pain, loss and death.

You may think considerations of the inner psychic realms of our human consciousness are irrelevant when facing a tsunami of rising sea levels, dying oceans, drought, floods, starvation and mass extinctions. But within whatever future we create to carry us through such challenges, these dimensions need to be understood by at least a few. Not everyone needs to be attuned to these realms, just as not everyone can climb on a roof to fix a leak, examine a tractor engine and fix it, cook tasty and nutritious meals or teach children with fun and laughter. But it all needs to be included. Otherwise the unconscious psycho-spiritual dynamics that have led to these catastrophes will be repeated.

One thing we've learned from history – we don't learn from history.

Recycling, signing petitions, becoming vegan, buying local, eating organic, planting trees, blocking roads, riding bikes, insulating houses, growing vegetables, sharing car journeys… these all matter. But when we collectively realise the apocalyptic destruction of our natural world is not going to be averted, external activism has to find new outlets.

We need to build alternatives to the current status quo and find new ways of being. Though all this needs to happen not only in the future, we need to connect with our profound and visceral love of life now. Our love for life can then begin immediately to transform our human consciousness.

What do you want for your birthday?

Oh ok - here's nothing.

Nothing matters more to me than discourse with highly evolved beetles such as myself.

It is an activism of a different kind to discover the non-rational wisdom of the body, to go beyond our individual egos and the collective ego of the world, to reclaim our animal instinctual natures, to attune to the sensitivities and perceptions we had to abandon to enter human culture, to honour the numinous and the mysterious, to enter realities beyond the frontiers of the intellect, to connect not only with the intellect and thought but also energy and feeling. As hopes for global action and material solutions disappear, an inner transformation of consciousness becomes a primary source of hope for building new lives.

If you haven't given up the old hopes yet, you soon will. Read the Climate Crisis section in the Guardian. Look at the trillions of dollars profits of the oil and gas industry. Find out about what's happening in the rainforest in Brazil, the Doomsday Glacier in the Antarctic and the ocean floor. Read global statistics on drought, floods, fires and soil depletion. Listen to the dire warnings and statistics coming from the UN.

Often we keep hoping simply because we don't know what else to do and the alternative looks like helpless despair. Yet depression and despair can be gateways into a deeper connection with what is real.

Through reality we discover what truly matters. And one of the most real experiences we ever encounter is the depth of our love for life, all life, not only our own.

Machiavelli says it's better to be feared than loved.

But I want people to be afraid of how much they love me.

Our instinctual love of life will not save the world, because it is not *of* the world, it is of life. But it will bring us to life. We will discover our brilliant minds are meant to serve life not dominate it. We will understand our division of life into separate things is a useful tool but no more than that. We will move away from a death-phobic culture that sacrifices life to stay alive and relax into the knowledge that though the individual body dies, our intellectual mind dies, tension dies, fear dies, the ego dies - our energy, consciousness and love live on in life forever. We will be so full of life we will know even death is life fulfilling itself. And because we love life we will surrender to this.

22 Instinctual Wisdom

> *To learn human language we had to abandon the universal language of all life, the instincts. As a result we can no longer communicate with the other members of our Earth family. We cannot hear what they have been trying to tell us for a long time, which is that although humans believe we belong to ourselves the deeper reality is that we belong to each other.*

There is a wisdom in the animal body we desperately need, though this wisdom is not about power, accumulating wealth or being 'someone'. But humanity's addiction to these things means we turn away from the answers waiting for us in the instincts and energies of the animal body. We want fame, fortune and power because we have been taught by profit-led corporate capitalism and mass media that to be ordinary is not enough. It doesn't help that our mega-technologies and identification with the thoughts of our intellectual minds have obliterated our awareness of other dimensions than material reality. And so we no longer have access to the only wisdom that can help us, the wisdom of life itself.

If I could talk, you would not understand me.

Life needs us to unearth our natural love of life because it will reconnect us with the reality that whatever our cultural sensitivities and intellectual powers, we are first and foremost living, breathing human Earth animals in an interconnectedness with all life. Without our animal body and its interconnectedness with the world wide web of life, humanity would not exist.

Animal instincts have evolved over millennia, not only to facilitate the survival of the individual, more importantly, to care for the survival of the ecosystem and the greater community of life. Victorian explorers like Charles Darwin and Alfred Wallace, projected their hierarchical patriarchy onto the animal kingdom and saw only the alpha males and the individual fight for survival. Their cultural blindness could not see the complex organisation of a pack or herd, the subtleties of matriarchal knowledge and power, the interdependence of different specialities within the group, the larger context of animal behaviour that protects the entire ecosystem, the surrender to the demands of the young and so on.

These complexities were invisible to the Victorian men who thought they ruled the world and left the hard but vital work of supporting everything to the 'lower orders', women, servants, paid employees, family retainers and the working classes, whose sweat and labour they took for granted.

Sometimes I wonder if I'm too arrogant –
then I remember I'm too good for that.

Similar arrogant oblivion is reflected these days in how we take the labour of other animals for granted. We remain ignorant of arenas where animal instincts are wiser than human thought, such as accessing non-rational awareness and sensitivities, surrendering without reservation to being alive, being completely immersed in the here and now, spontaneous moment to moment and totally committed to being alive. Most significantly, where we have spectacularly failed, animal instincts protect the biosphere as well as themselves to preserve the dynamic balance of the whole ecosystem.

Evolution is not dependent solely on the fight for survival of each individual. For a start, the existence of many species depends upon the survival of other species. For example, in dry seasons, elephants use their tusks to dig for water that provides relief for other thirsty animals. They create gaps in forest vegetation that give space for new plants to grow and smaller animals to find new paths through the forest.

Parrotfish maintain coral reefs by eating and removing microalgae, which otherwise would cover the reef, hinder its growth and eventually kill it.

Fungi create vast underground networks called the mycelium, or wood wide web. Their arm-like membranes build symbiotic communication networks that connect the whole ecosystem and enable individual trees, bushes and plants to communicate with each other.

Ants are tiny but all over the world they dig tunnels, aerate the earth and recycle nutrients, keeping the soil rich and healthy for plant growth without chemical fertilisers or irrigation. In fact recent research has found that ants have an even higher efficacy than pesticides, and at lower costs. (Proceedings of Royal Society B. D Anjos et al August 2022.)

Humans neglect this wider reality in part because we are identified with our minds and our identities as separate individuals. Yet our intellect allows us to access only one level of reality. The deeper river of existence is an energetic bio-interconnectedness between all living creatures. Our apparent separateness is a temporary phenomenon on the surface, like a wave is not the ocean. We are so identified with the wave we have forgotten the vastness of the ocean.

Am I a drop in the ocean? No, you're the ocean in a drop.

Though our minds have forgotten, our genetic memory holds the living knowledge that the other animals are our kin, our ancestors, and that we have within us this same instinctual intelligence. Our brilliant but blinkered logical minds have led us into this eco-crisis, they will not therefore alone be able to save us from it. We need our clever minds to work in tandem with our instinctual intelligence and together, with mutual respect, enable us to navigate the dark waters soon to be engulfing us. But first the intellectual mind must recognise its limitations.

Our individualistic materialist minds tend to be strongly focused on the concrete and neglect the formless. F. D. Peat interviewed the Blackfoot Tribe in North America who described this kind of mind as 'Hard, logical, and forceful, confined to the practical, concrete reality. It rejects all experience that appears out of the ordinary. The Native mind does not erect barriers to an extended reality. People negotiate with the world of spirits and form alliances with the powers that animate the universe. The Indigenous world is alive.'

Modern humans need to do some soul-searching.

Let's hope they find one.

Indigenous minds are alive to the world of energy and not confined to what can be defined and explained. We also need to connect with these dimensions. The deeper truths of life reveal themselves only when our minds are open to the formless energy fields of existence. This is hard for our western minds attached to the power of analysis and logic.

Another difficulty is we are very identified with our intellectual minds and are therefore afraid of the realities beyond it. We would simply be curious about altered states of consciousness otherwise. As a culture we are so afraid of these other dimensions we have made psychedelic plants, a major tool for shamanic journeys to other dimensions, illegal.

In order to navigate the Anthropocene extinction we need to explore our relationship with the invisible energy fields of life, including the great unknown of death. Otherwise we will carry into the future the same toxic fears that have poisoned what was once a paradise. Not that Earth was ever a perfect idyll; it is a real and embodied paradise and therefore includes death.

If we face our fears and open our hearts to life we will discover a different kind of paradise, one that also embraces the Serpent - death. After all Eden was home to snakes and reptiles long before mammals arrived on the scene.

Some are wise - some are other-wise.

23 Let's Talk About Death.

> *An animal will fight to the death for life, but not because it is afraid to die, because it is committed to life. When we humans die, it is more complex. We know that death ends our individual life. To the degree we are identified with our separate existence rather than our interconnectedness with others, this creates anxieties in us that other animals do not have. Yet death is intrinsic to life. Without death life would have no meaning.*

You could argue that exploring the psycho-spiritual dimensions of our humanity is irrelevant when our survival is threatened and the primary focus has to be shelter, food and warmth. Yes there is a hierarchy of needs and you cannot afford to arrange flowers when your house is burning down. But we will run into trouble without at least some connection with these invisible realms. Everything must be engaged, children, buildings, animals, housing, cooking, cleaning, farming, and our psychological and spiritual health – and this includes coming to terms with death. Especially when we experience the disintegration of our world and death will be all around us.

In order to deal even remotely effectively with the disintegration of the world-wide food web, the collapse of biodiversity, the desertification of what was fertile land, the horrors of a mass extinction and the loss of so much life in all directions, one thing we have to do is come to terms with death.

'There is but one freedom, to put oneself right with death. After that everything is possible.' Albert Camus

Death is part of life. It *is* life. Which is why our terror of death needs to be addressed because it is a disguised terror of life. With this in mind let's explore our relationship with death because it is intrinsic to our relationship with life and whatever is our future.

I've just bought a coffin.	That's the last thing you need.

Love and consciousness are the most intimate and self-evident realities while also being two of the most transcendent and indefinable. Yet neither life nor love nor consciousness would have meaning without death. Death renders life unbearably meaningful.

The only certainty in life is death. There may be few correspondences between the lives of a Chinese politician, a native of the Amazonian jungle, a Wall St banker and a single mother in a Glasgow housing estate, but they have one thing in common - whatever our lives, we all die. Whether we believe death is oblivion, an awakening, an ending or a transformation, death itself is a reality we cannot avoid. And whether we look for the meaning of death in our human earthly existence or seek meaning in a transcendental dimension beyond this realm, death ensures that each moment matters.

All creatures are cremated equal.

We might think we want to live forever but what would happen when we had done it all, lived it all, experienced it all, and yet continued to be alive? We would have no future other than a relentless banality of boredom and meaninglessness with no challenge or creativity and nothing left to explore and discover. We would soon long for the release of death.

Many traditions and cultures throughout history have understood that life and death are not antagonistic opposites but interdependent realities in which each takes its significance from the other. The Sufi secret for wisdom was to know that 'this too will pass.' The Zen teaching said to guarantee enlightenment in one lifetime was to live as if death would arrive the next moment. Jack Kerouac's advice on how to connect with our creativity was: 'accept loss forever.'

These perspectives recognise that our place in the cosmos, the evolution of our consciousness and our psycho-spiritual destinies are to be found in death as much as in life.

The animal body itself does not fear death. An animal will fight to the death for life, but not because it is afraid to die, because it is committed to life. When we humans die, it is more complex. We know that death ends our individual life. To the degree we are identified with our separate existence rather than our interconnectedness with others, this creates anxieties in us that other animals do not have. Except when they spend a lot of time with humans.

Are you worried about dying?

Nah. It's not going to happen in my lifetime.

On death our separation from the whole is ended, duality is dissolved and we return to the oceanic one-ness of all life. This process unfolds whether we surrender to our death or go out fighting. Ultimately, of course, there is only the surrender. But when we know our death is part of life's evolution rather than merely the ending of a life, then our death will be less of a struggle. We can simply live our death as we have lived our life.

The greatest good is not eternal life, it is to live one's life and die one's death in love and freedom. What greater good can there be than this? The wisdom of the body with its direct experience of our lives, loves, freedoms and deaths shows us that death is not the enemy after all. Our fear of death is far more dangerous.

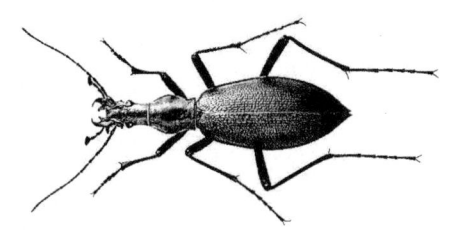

In the beginning was the void, then God said let there be light.
There was still the void but you could see it better.

24 Life, Death & the Mystery

> *We think we are separate individuals but that is not the whole story. We are profoundly interconnected and interdependent with the rest of life. Death is intrinsic to the flow of this vast river because death is the means through which life continually renews itself. Life without death would have no meaning. Even a Mass Extinction Event has meaning for the evolution of life.*

Our origins lie deep in history. The greatest story ever told, the story of life on Earth, is written in our bones.

A single fertilised cell grows through binary division into a complex organism. As the embryo grows it passes through the many stages of the evolution and in our nine months in the womb, embryonic shadows of gills, wings, webbed feet, tails and horns emerge and fade. The history of our biological ancestors lives on in us.

The interconnectedness of life is not only historical - all creatures are in a continual process of becoming each other. 'Eat or be eaten' is the law of the jungle. The life force of the carrot becomes the life force of the rabbit who eats it, this becomes the life force of the owl who catches the rabbit and then the life force of the fox who eats the owl who ate the rabbit who ate the carrot. Predator and prey continually merge.

From one perspective, we *are* each other.

Vegetarians eat vegetables - I'm a humanitarian.

Each living creature is unique, separate and distinct, like individual waves on the ocean. At the same time we are interdependent, interconnected and continually becoming each other, like the ocean itself. The idea that our bodies are separate and belong solely to ourselves is just one story; another is that our body belongs to life - and life is one body in which we are all members of each other. As 'The Destroyer of Lies' in an Apache legend tells us, 'This earth is my body. The sky is my body. The seasons are my body. The water is my body. These are all my body.'

The vast communion of all life is not an abstract or conceptual idea, it is a living reality, a visceral experience. Our animal bodies 'know' in a different way from the intellectual knowing of our conscious minds that every living animal, plant, fungus and creature from the seven kingdoms of life, have their origins in this river and one day will dissolve back into its oceanic oneness. This great river of life has been given many names. Gaia, Tao, Dharma, Dreamtime, Prana, Chi, the quantum energy field, God, Moksha, Wakan Taka, Ein Sof, Anima Mundi, Shiva and Shakti, Kosmos, The Force… Yet whatever we call this vast flow of life, it is the only sacred entity in existence.

What do you want with your burger?   I'm a Buddhist - make me one with everything.

The flow of life through all living creatures continually renews itself through death. Whether death is of an individual, a species or an ecosystem, it is intrinsic to life. Even Mass Extinctions play their role in the continuity and evolution of life.

Despite the fact that death is essential to life, we rarely explore its significance and meaning. Naturally when struggling to build our lives, create a home, pay the bills and bring up children, we are not going to think much about how one day all this will end. Yet to navigate the deaths of the eco-apocalypse we need to be able to engage the reality of death because it will be happening around us in all directions.

The more we understand death, the less afraid of it we will be. The less afraid of death we become, the more we will be able to engage life.

Better to make our peace with death and dying now; it will by much harder in the panic and terror of apocalyptic destruction.

As historians well know, an event is never truly over; it lives on in unfolding futures forever. The great mystery of death, even the mass deaths of extinctions, is that all that has ever lived, lives on, in some form or other, in life forever. We enrich future life with whatever legacy we create while alive. This makes our lives profoundly meaningful; we are creating future life in the way we live.

Why should I care about future generations - what have they ever done for me?

All life forms instinctively know how precious life is, which is why creatures continually seek nourishment, care for their young, move away from danger and so on. Because of our separation from and control over the spontaneous instinctual flow of life through our bodies, we humans have become consciously aware of this. You have to separate from something to then look back and 'know' it consciously. Though with that knowledge comes responsibility. To navigate the future intelligently we need an awareness of how precious all life is, not only our own.

It helps to understand that without death life would have no meaning and that though death is an inconsolable loss, it is what renders life so precious. This understanding can enable us to face the mass deaths ahead with less fear. Especially as being afraid of death translates into being afraid of life and we need to expand into our love of life rather than shrink away afraid.

Death is the gift of our lives back to life as we leave. Love can be defined as the gift of oneself. This means love, as well as death, is at the heart of the mystery of life. Our love of life, all the more conscious because of our alienation from life, together with our appreciation of the mystery of death, will then play a key role in our navigation of the eco-apocalypse.

Eternity is not in the future, we're living in it now.

So is this heaven or hell?

25 Eros & Thanatos

> *Death makes life so precious, our love makes us willing to die so that those we love can live. This means however powerful death is, in the end, love is more powerful. Eros is greater than Thanatos. Love can therefore offer us a way to navigate the vast dying of the Anthropocene extinction.*

Death ends a life but not the relationship we have with the one who has died. Wherever we locate dead people and animals, whether in heaven, in our hearts, in our memories, in the dark energy of the universe, in the void of non-being or in the cosmic energy fields of existence outside time and space, our love for them continues beyond their deaths. Love survives death. Eros is greater than Thanatos. In the future, when we are witnessing deaths around us in all directions, our love of life will become even more vital.

Do you have concrete evidence of life after death?

No, very few souls are made of concrete.

It is not our fantastic power and glory that lead us to love; it is our vulnerable and ordinary humanity. We tend to think we have to be amazing or brilliant to be loved, to be successful and powerful for our love to mean much, but to love and loved requires frail and imperfect mammalian bodies that bleed and hurt and die.

We may be able to shock and awe through our power and dazzle with our brilliance, but our imperfections, insecurities, needs, vulnerabilities, inadequacies, failures, mistakes and existential anxieties are what foster and create love. We wouldn't need love if we were already perfect - though some adoration and worship might not go amiss. But that's not love.

Death cannot destroy love. What death cannot destroy is eternal. Love is eternal. The love that opens us up to life beyond our individual survival does not come from a far away God in his heaven; it evolves down here, on Earth, forged in the struggle of warm-blooded mammals who must love one another or die. In the Christian myth, even the greatest God of them all had to become human and die in order to create the love the cosmos needs to fulfil itself. The mortal is the source of the immortal, not the other way round. We bring into being that which survives death through that which dies.

For goodness sake keep sinning –
otherwise Jesus died for nothing.

Each of us came into being through a man and a woman making love. Whoever we are and whatever we create has its primal origins in the lovemaking of our parents. The whole world of our cities, machines, libraries, universities, hospitals, factories, roads, airports, ships, the vast infrastructure of our global civilisation has its original source in humanity's animal bodies. Animals, fish, birds, reptiles, creatures everywhere also come into being through the feeling bodies of soft animal tissue and the tender organs of a creature-hood that bleeds, suffers and dies.

Yet another paradox, one of the greatest: death makes life so precious, our love makes us willing to die so that those we love can live. Love can therefore offer us a way to navigate the vast dying of the Anthropocene extinction, even as our hearts are breaking.

I love life more than myself – but don't make me prove it.

Though we are responsible for creating the love we need. We not only make the love that makes us, literally through making sexual love, we also create love in many other ways. When we give ourselves to someone beyond our individual ego, when we dare to be real and vulnerable with each other, when we are willing to suffer for something beyond our own survival, when
we dare to truly love a situation, a possibility or creature other than ourselves, when we care for children, animals and all creatures that feel and breathe the same air as us, when we walk in mountains and gaze at the wonder and beauty all around us, when we rage and weep at what we've done to life on Earth, or whatever is our particular way to express and experience our love of life, we are contributing to a continually evolving energy-field of love that not even death can destroy.

I'm working on a cure for natural causes.

Love may not be all we need, but we all need love. Through daring to love we create the death-less. Another paradox: humanity's alienation from life, the source of this tragedy, is exactly what creates a consciousness and love of life that will carry us through it.

When confronted by the deaths of the Anthropocene extinction our love of life can help us navigate the heartbreak and loss and come to the deeper meaning of what is happening. And it doesn't matter how you live your life, or what are your successes and failures, or what tribe you belong to, as long as there's love in it.

Suwoop man, wassup blood, cool with the homies?

Yeah souljah, gangsta it up innit and shit.

26   Life Without Death Has No Meaning

> *We try to deny death, not because we are committed to life, because we are terrified of death. We then find ourselves in a fight with nature. But a species at war with nature is at war with itself, and so we live in fear not only of ourselves we are at war with life - because we are terrified of death.*

Other animals do not live in a future where tomorrow casts a dark shadow over today because all tomorrows hold the threat of death. They live in the moment in blissful ignorance that death annihilates the individual creature. We humans hold this dreadful knowledge, which separates us further from other animals. Yet this knowledge is the crucible within which the soul of humanity is born. Love and death are inextricably entangled with the very consciousness that makes us human.

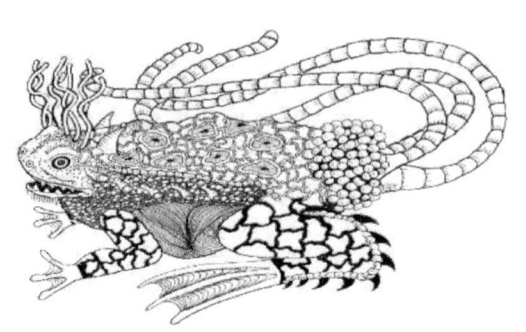

I'm not afraid of death, I just don't want to be there when it happens.

For many years I couldn't see what humans contributed to the natural world other than danger and destruction. In my search to understand all this I took part in some Ayahuasca ceremonies. They were profound and life-altering experiences that are impossible to describe. I can only describe them as profound meetings with an alien non-human plant intelligence that led to startling and potent revelations.

The Ayahuasca vine, also called the Vine of Death, revealed to me that through the anguish of knowing we will die, we create a consciousness and love that nature needs to fulfil itself. She told me that the whole cosmos needs humanity to make our contribution of love and consciousness to existence.

We also are nature. It is our human nature to be divided against ourselves. Nature needs at least one species to alienate it from itself in order to give birth to the consciousness that knows itself, life, and therefore death. The Ayahuasca showed me that we have a major role to play in the drama of existence after all, in the creation of the conscious soul of the universe, which is a fulfilment and meaning for nature as well as ourselves. Through us the universe is becomes conscious of itself.

Reality is for people who can't handle drugs.

Have you been at those fermenting apples again?

Life is sacred, not many of us would argue with that, but what renders life sacred is not religious ritual or belief. The source of the sacred is nature not a heavenly transcendental realm of light beings and angels. The spirit must arrive in the body, not the body ascend to the spirit. Then the body will take care of our living and dying so that the spirit, when it is released, has true soul.

Our souls are not ready-made entities we are born with, pre-existing beyond the turbulence of life and love on Earth. We create our souls through how we live. A soul is forged in the struggles and surrenders of life in the almost unbearable human predicament of being a creature in conflict with itself who knows one day it will die. Another paradox: Our anguish of living with the terrible knowledge of death also gives us our conscious and soulful joy at being alive. We cannot have one without the other.

I intend to live forever – so far so good.

We humans experience both life and death and are conscious of both life and death. This conscious awareness is where humanity cooks up its soul. The existential anguish of knowing we are alive, and therefore will die, impels us to create something that will survive our death. Something that cannot die, such as love, freedom, justice, beauty, truth, a work of art, food recipes, wisdom, happy children, an Olympic gold medal, whatever…

Our awareness of death forces us to create a soul so that when our spirit is released from the material world it is more than a mere idea; it has presence and energy – whether that reality is as a memory in the hearts and minds of people who knew us, a vibration in the cosmic energy fields, an aspect of the invisible dark energy that maintains existence or part of a mystery beyond our comprehension.

The Ayahuasca spirit showed me that we humans, with our conscious knowledge of death and therefore our knowledge of how precious life is, must create a love of life that is greater than death. Humanity is responsible for creating this aspect of the geo-soul. Other life forms have different destinies. But whatever the species, we all create the energies that contribute to the soul of the universe in and through the animal body. This is because the animal body loves life enough to suffer all experience in its entirety, with no protection and no ego to interfere with that totality. And whatever our intellectual minds think or believe about life and death, it is the animal body that experiences them. The crucible of consciousness is experience not thought.

I may be in the mud but I'm looking at the stars.

Me too – where the hell has the roof gone?

Our lives give meaning to our deaths, not what happens after we die. We forge our souls on Earth, nowhere else. We cook up wisdom and compassion, laughter and consciousness, beauty and meaning, freedom and love through our struggles, conflicts and anguish here in the mud of life on Earth. The after-life is simply the consequence of how we have lived this life. What matters is not what happens when we die, that will take care of itself - how we live is what matters.

Yet another paradox: the very creature, whose demise is the definition of death, no heartbeat, no breath, no electrical activity in the cortex, is also the creature that is a gateway into what is beyond that death – more life.

My death will be the end of my life. Yet from another perspective my life is not really 'mine' and never has been. The Ayahuasca showed me that 'I' am the temporary guardian of an array of energies, that's all. Death is the transition from 'my' life to 'our' life. Ultimately 'my' life was, is and always will be 'our' life because we belong to each other as much as to ourselves. From this perspective, there is therefore no death, only more life.

After the Ayahuasca spirit had shown me more things than I can write about here, I bowed down to her to honour and thank her. She then bowed to me, to honour and thank humanity for our lonely exile from the oneness of nature and the conscious awareness of life and death this gives us. No other creature, plant, fungi or life form has this wonderful and dreadful knowledge. We took leave of each other with mutual respect and gratitude.

I'm rooting for you, heart and soil.

27 The Field

> *All things die. The demise of our vast and great civilisation was always going to happen. Yet our lives continue to influence life beyond our individual deaths through the action of energy-fields. We are playing our part in a mystery beyond our comprehension.*

The reality of the climate crisis and the 6th Mass Extinction is beginning to reveal itself. Just tonight the BBC news reported that one third of Pakistan is under water from floods and millions are destitute. The next news item was of the drought in Spain and elsewhere in Europe that will seriously affect the world's supply of olive oil, sunflower oil and tomatoes. Then there was the war in Ukraine causing a lack of grain leading to starvation in Africa and higher food prices everywhere. Humans, animals and plants dying due to loss of habitat, industrial pollution, mass migration, global warming, rising sea levels, melting glaciers, ocean anoxia and a collapse of biodiversity is going to get worse.

It might help us cope with the suffering to know that the very human behaviour that caused this global tragedy is something that was always going to happen. Our conscious appreciation of life has been born out of our dislocation from life. The seeds of our destruction of life lie right at the core of our greatest gift to life. It might enable us to face the future with less devastating remorse to know that the demise of our great civilisation and culture, though utterly tragic, is not only to a large extent inevitable - it has a meaning for future life.

People keep banging on about the apocalypse as if there's no tomorrow.

Biologists cannot explain how a single fertilised egg can grow through binary fission into a creature with arms and legs, organs and nervous system, nor how a flock of starlings can fly in a murmuration with precision and responsiveness way beyond the reaction times of individual birds. Even how evolution itself happened is a mystery. And too how existence came to exist in the first place is unknown, let alone how it came to life.

Rupert Sheldrake has suggested one explanation lies in the shaping power of energy fields. Physicists too say the more they look into the nature of reality the more they discover everything is energy. From the macro level of astronomy through to the micro level of quantum physics, scientists talk about energy fields, vibrations, strings of energy, quantum entanglement, dark energy and so on. Einstein himself wrote, 'The field is the only reality.'

From this perspective we can view the processes of life as unfolding within a vast transcendentally interconnected energy field. This field of energy can be described as a force-field outside the dimensions of space and time that acts on and shapes reality as it unfolds into its many dimensions of form. After all, people far better equipped than me have linked the theoretical models of modern physics to ancient mystical maps of the universe.

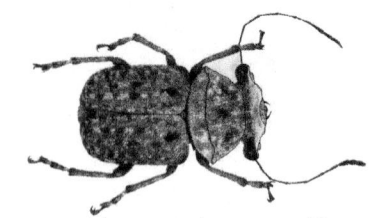

I get quantum theory – dreams stuff is made of.

As our great mammalian cycle of life dies, the next great cycle of life on Earth will come to life. If we look at life from this cosmic perspective, as humans become extinct, the consciousness and love we have created over millennia will be released into the energy fields of existence. These energies can then shape life from another dimension of existence.

All the love, wisdom, beauty, consciousness, freedom, creative dreaming and everything of soul that we have collectively generated while alive, will be available to shape future life. And from the vastness of a transcendentally interconnected energy field, we will continue to play our part in the creation of a vast energy field of love and consciousness that some might call God. Though I prefer the word Life.

So the universe implodes – no matter.

Though these are things beyond our comprehension. This is merely an attempt to point towards a mystery that cannot be expressed in words. Perhaps only dancers, poets, artists and musicians can hint at it, while wild creatures simply live it.

When we gaze into the eyes of an unafraid wild animal, we see directly into the soul of the Earth. We need to connect with that geo-soul within us and play our human part in creating it. The soul is not a thing; it is an energy. We are not objects; we are phenomena. Life is not a problem to be solved; it is a mystery to be lived. Being alive is to be experienced, not just survived. What is happening is not merely a series of events linked in a cause-effect chain, it is a transcendentally interconnected energy field that unfolds in many dimensions simultaneously.

If we are to live through the apocalyptic times ahead with any degree of love, freedom, truth, wisdom, integrity, compassion, understanding, generosity, happiness, creativity, or however we describe whatever is our particular meaning and purpose - we have to start living here in whatever way speaks to us.

'Ask the animals, and they will teach you, speak to the earth, and it will teach you.' Job 12:7-10

Don't give up on your dreams.   No, that's why I sleep so much.

28 Fear of Fear

> *One of the most universal myths is that when we die our exile ends and we return home to the source, Nirvana, heaven... whatever name we use. Yet we cannot really answer the question, what happens when we die? This is because what is being addressed is a person not an event and we must each answer it in our own way. Our life is our answer. Just as we each have to each find our own understanding of the current eco-catastrophe.*

Each atom in our bodies is billions of years old. Hydrogen, the most common element in the universe and a major element in our bodies, was produced in the big bang 13.7bn years ago. Heavier atoms, such as carbon and oxygen, were forged in stars between 7bn and 12bn years ago and blasted across space when the stars exploded. Each of us is composed of the energies, forces and material of the universe. Our bodies are truly stardust.

Everything's made of electrons, protons and neutrons.

Don't forget the morons.

We might name what constitutes us as matter, stardust, clouds of glory, cosmic consciousness, chemical elements, DNA, quantum entanglements, spirit or whatever. Yet however we describe them, these materials and energies combine temporarily to form an entity we each call 'me'. When we die those energies are released to become elements of another entity, energy, existence or reality.

Perhaps some of them become part of another being that calls itself 'me'. But it will not be this 'me', the one I call myself. That dies. Though not all of 'me' dies. One of the most universal myths is that when we die our exile ends and we return home to the source, God, the Dreaming, Nirvana, heaven... whatever name we use. This belief has been called the 'perennial philosophy' because it has been found in every society and culture in some form or other. It is at the heart of all the world's major religions and found in the cultures of indigenous people all over the world.

Perhaps we need such myths to ease the existential anxiety that comes with our dreadful knowledge of death - that whatever we do, however we live and whoever we become, one day we will be gone. We need to believe there must be more than annihilation else what's the point of struggling so hard to survive?

Or perhaps they are attempts to ease the anguish of exile from our instinctual home in nature by seeking a home in an after-life. Or perhaps it is simply that without an understanding that human life has significance and meaning beyond itself, our struggles and death appear nothing but pointless pains with no redemptive meaning whatsoever.

Life's hard.   Compared to what?

Yet such myths are more than opiates for the soul. Myths and maps of what happens when we die place our human suffering in its rightful place in the cosmos and give meaning to our anguish. They help us go beyond a relentless fight for survival into living lives in which we create beauty out of chaos, wisdom from suffering, justice from conflict, mutual understanding from war, and so on. From this perspective, the primary function of myths is not to inform us of the facts of another reality or to tell us what will happen when we die, it is to enable us to live well.

The problems arise when we confuse metaphor with fact and think that myths of death are speaking of actual realities in the same way science speaks of our material world. We then try to work out which version is the right one. We dissolve into a blissful light where all is revealed. We develop an astral body and choose our next re-incarnation. We lounge about on clouds with our ancestors. St Peter meets us at the pearly gates and gives us a VIP pass or shakes his head at our muddy trainers. But if we think such descriptions of what happens when we die are describing real situations or events, we miss the point. They are symbolic descriptions and metaphors not facts. Myths are truths because they illuminate our humanity, but they are not facts.

Stop telling lies about me.   When you stop telling truths about me

The question of what happens when we die therefore has to be understood as myth not science, truth not fact, metaphor not actuality, energy not form. Language is a useful tool when dealing with material reality and objects separated in space and time, but when it comes to talking about energies, fields, quantum entanglement, events in realms beyond the space-time continuum, it is limited. There is no answer to the question, what is death? This is because what is being addressed is a person, not the event. We will each answer it differently. Our life is our answer.

I believe in karma. So when I do bad things to people it's because they deserve it.

What is life? What is death? What is the meaning of the Anthropocene Mass Extinction? These are questions that cannot be answered by our intellect; they can only be answered by how we live. So how do we live through the current eco-crisis and the vast deaths of the 6th Mass Extinction? One option is to pretend it's not happening and live in denial. Another is to get lost in panic and fear. Another is to fall into a nihilistic despair and turn to drink and drugs to escape. Another is to take responsibility for what is happening, engage it creatively and bring all the love and intelligence of our humanity to bear on it.

What would prevent us taking the only option with any hope is our terror of the deaths we will be witnessing.

Death will be a potent and unavoidable part of our experience when the natural world disintegrates around us. Whatever kind of ark we build to carry us through the storm, whatever principles we evolve within our various communities, whether alone or with others, we will have to deal with death. In this process we will be forced to confront all the fears we have around death else we will be lost in panic and terror unable to offer consciousness or love to the unfolding tragedy.

Many things can help us, an extended understanding of who we are, a respect for instinctual intelligence, a grounding in the energy of our bodies, the realisation that we love life more than we had any idea and so on. But we must also encounter whatever fears we have projected onto death and release them, else when the storm hits, we will be full of fear not love. And though love may not be all we need, we all need love. It is what will enable us to build our ark.

I want to build an ark.   I noah a guy who can help you.

29   Releasing Fear

> *To release our fear of death it helps to understand that death is the end of our power over life and is a surrender to life. We are not really afraid of death itself, we are afraid of our experience, ultimately our experience of ourselves. Death reveals the truth of ourselves to ourselves. The 6th Mass Extinction is revealing to us the truth of life on Earth.*

When we die we lose our grounding in life. Death is the end of our sensual experience, our sight, hearing, taste, smell, touch and feeling are all gone. There is no more breathing, eating, sleeping, dancing, making love or doing anything. Death is the end of our separate existence and our individual identity. Death is the end of literally every 'thing' and all that 'matters'. Death is the end of our intellectual minds and its capacity for language and abstract thought, the end of our defensiveness, control and ego, and the end of our alienation, tension and existential anxiety.

Yet all this loss may not be the painful tragedy the individual self imagines.

Death takes your breath away.

Death involves the release of our energy from the controlling patterns of our ego, our identity, our conditioned mind and the chronic patterns of tension in the body. Our control over the flow of life through our bodies is to prevent what we fear from happening. Death is a relaxation of that control and this triggers fears of whatever we've been trying to keep at bay; but it is also a relaxation of that fear. Which is why the dissolution of the ego on death may not be what we fear at all. What we are really afraid of are our fears themselves.

Until we deal with our fears, face them, resolve and release them, we project them into the future. We imagine scenarios that might happen when what we really fear has already happened. A burned child dreads fire, another is cautiously curious. This is why we each fear different things. Our fears from the past, such as childhood fears of being overwhelmed, annihilated, helpless, losing what we love, being abandoned, left in pain, alone, bullied, attacked, hurt, impotent or whatever, are ultimately projected onto the furthest point away from us in the future – our death. Death receives the projections of all of our unresolved fears.

What are you afraid of?   I was afraid you'd ask that.

On death we encounter all our unresolved fears of life because when we are dying, there is no more future to project our fears onto and therefore no escape from them. This is the death agony. We think we are afraid of dying but really we are afraid of our fear. Yet another paradox: death contains everything we fear yet death itself is nothing to be afraid of.

In the first stage of death we lose our conscious minds and our senses. In the second we encounter our unresolved fears. In the third we encounter the truth of ourselves. In this stage the energy that was contained and controlled by our ego is released and who we truly are, rather than the imagined self the ego has constructed, is revealed. Our magnificence and meanness, our hatred and joy, our love and our distortions, all become apparent, because there is no controller left to hide, repress or deny our true reality. We become the pure energy of ourselves. And this energy truth-body becomes apparent for us to experience and know.

Are you a knight in shining armour or an idiot wrapped in tin foil?

I'm a tin angel.

Each death is unique because we die as we have lived and how we have lived our lives is unique. Yet every death, like the life that precedes it, is a profound meeting with the reality of who and what we are.

Many find the revelations that emerge as we die so frightening they turn to medication to numb the distress it causes, but that may not be the escape we hope for.

According to many traditions and myths of death there is ultimately no way to avoid the truth of oneself - it can happen after our death if not before.

The Tibetan Book of the Dead says we have 49 days after death in which to encounter our fears (demons) and create our truth-body. In the ancient Egyptian Book of the Dead, our good and bad deeds are weighed in a balance to reveal our next destiny. Christians say we have our time in purgatory to face the truth of our lives and digest our shadow. In the Hindu mythology the soul of the deceased can take up to a year to reach the final judgement about whether your reincarnation is as a beetle, a giraffe, a daisy or a human. In the humanistic tradition death is a reckoning with ourselves, as there is only one moral authority, that of our own integrity. Yet whatever the mythology, there is an almost universal sense that death reveals who you really are, to yourself if no one else.

What do liars do when they're dead?   Lie still.

What realities will the deaths of the eco-apocalypse and the mass extinction reveal about life on Earth? Maybe that life on Earth with all its anarchic chaos, profound vulnerabilities and real embodied love has a part to play in an even bigger story. And although we will be suffering, there are dimensions even in the midst of this eco-catastrophe, where life is fulfilling itself through us. Maybe understanding it has all been of far more significance than just a tragedy will help.

30   Dimensions of Being

> *We need a modern narrative of death that speaks to our current culture. In our modern individualised culture we each contain a multitude of selves and each of those dies differently. Death is not therefore a singular event, it is a process that unfolds simultaneously in many dimensions. Understanding the complexities of death will help us navigate the vast deaths of the Anthropocene Extinction.*

To help us navigate the deaths we will encounter in the on-going mass extinction and climate chaos we need a modern narrative of death, one that does not merely turn to mediaeval myths or ancient eastern culture for answers but is rooted in our current understandings of human nature and the workings of the universe. Our culture's primary narrative of death is that it is a tragic annihilation to be avoided at all costs, even when that cost is life on Earth. We do not even allow people the freedom and autonomy to choose their own death when they are terminally ill and in pain.

We need conversations about death that embrace contemporary understandings of life because these will uncover new dimensions to death. And we need this to help us face the inevitable mass deaths of this eco-crisis with something other than denial, blind panic or violence. Which matters because even if we have managed to build an ark in the form of a relatively self sufficient community, we will still have to deal with the deaths around us, including many humans as well as animals and plants.

'Death brings us into absolute and passionate presence with all that is here, that is natural, that is love.' Rainer Maria Rilke

The trouble with conversations about death is they're always with people who are still alive.

I find it helps to understand that death is not a singular event; it is a process that unfolds simultaneously in many dimensions. In our modern individualised culture we each contain a multitude of selves, sub-personalities and energies. Each aspect and energy that was part of the 'I' that is me, dies in its own way. So what might happen when we die?

- Some energies of who and what we are live on in the memories of those who knew us.
- Some parts of us return to Earth and the molecules reconstituted in a pebble, a beetle or the dust on the wing of a moth.
- Some parts may remain connected to whatever or whoever we love until they too die.
- Some parts are lost forever, have ended, are gone.
- Other parts, such as our wisdom, consciousness and love, may become part of the energy fields that shape nature and reality from an overarching transcendentally interconnected energy field outside time and space.
- Some energies may remain connected with life on Earth perhaps as psychic elements of movements for justice or revenge.

- Some energies may remain forever connected with our families and those we love as a disembodied presence within their hearts and memories.
- Some energies, such as our fear, greed, envy, resentment and ignorance, may return to earth to be embodied within another ego-I in order to resolve themselves.
- Some energies may return to earth and incarnate as love and wisdom in order to bring light to the darkness that is here.
- Some parts may become elements of the archetypes, memes or zeitgeist that form aspects of our human culture and psyche.
- Some energies may return to the source and dissolve into the oneness, God, the light, whatever name we give the great mystery, never to emerge again.

I tried to hang myself with a bungee cord and kept having near death experiences.

Whether death is oblivion, a return to the turmoil of life or a dissolving back into the source, God, eternal peace or Nirvana, or a bit of each of these, depends completely upon how we have lived. The 'I' who asks these questions dies. Anne dies. I am a temporary phenomenon, a meeting in time and space of an array of energies who came together for a while but one day will disband.

Yet this life, lived in this body, in this particular time and space, has eternal implications. Anne, the person, dies. She ceases to exist. 'Anne-ness' lives on in a multitude of energies and forms.

Just as each culture will arrive at its own understanding of what is death, we each individually live our own life and die our own death. There is no absolute meaning of life or death other than the ones we create, because we *are* the meaning. One thing we can say about all death is the more we have given ourselves to life, in whatever way has meaning for us, the more profound will be our death.

Just when I worked out the meaning of life, they changed it.

We may never find a meaning in the eco-catastrophe of the Anthropocene Extinction. It might have no meaning beyond just the experience of inconsolable loss and tragedy. Yet our struggle with its implications for life will yield understandings that can help us navigate it. A tragedy of this order has never happened to humanity before so we can no longer turn to the wisdom of the ancients and those who have gone before us for answers. We have to create the meaning ourselves.

The understanding that helps me is that when we die we give all that we have created in and through our lives on Earth back to existence as we leave. This is our unique contribution to the whole, to life, to eternity, to the source from which all things flow and into which all things return. In this way we each play our part in the great mystery of existence. Together we create what created us. And on death we become it.

Let's ruin each other beyond repair and blame love.

31   A Return to Paradise

> *Love was born in the warm hearts of mammals that bonded with their young. This bonding evolved into a complex love that embodied empathy, compassion and altruistic kindness. The animal body is the original source of all love. A disembodied heavenly being or God has little to do with it. The embodied love in the animal body is the force we need to navigate the fast approaching eco-apocalypse.*

The industrial military complex is not going to disarm itself. The corporate world is not going to suddenly put life before profits. Religions can offer nothing because at their core is an anti-life belief that this life is merely a prelude to what really matters – the after-life. Much scientific research is now funded by the military, pharmaceutical companies and the corporate world and has consequently become part of the problem not the solution. There is almost universal denial that our addiction to seeking happiness through owning things is devastating the natural world. Campaigning, demonstrating, signing petitions, direct action, glueing ourselves to roads, meditating to raise our vibrational levels, chanting under a full moon or any other method through which we hope to escape the cataclysmic future facing us are not going to avert the eco-apocalypse either. Our world is ending.

What will people say in the future about the lack of action on the eco-crisis?   Nothing.

181

This irreversible devastation is an apocalyptic tragedy, yet life itself will continue. In the continual cycle of life renewing itself through death, new life forms will evolve. During the K/T Extinction Event 65 million years ago, the dinosaurs died out and mammals were able to evolve from a tiny mouse-like creature just a few inches long into the magnificent biodiversity of the great mammals such as lions, elephants, wolves, whales, gorillas, and humans. Mammals differed from the fish, reptiles, insects and dinosaurs that preceded them in several key aspects.

They were warm-blooded creatures. Rather than simply seeking the warmth from the sun, mammals created and maintained heat inside their bodies. But this was not the only difference. Fish and insects give birth to thousands at a time. From the very beginning, these tiny creatures struggle to survive on their own. Very few reach maturity. Mammals on the other hand give birth to only a few offspring each time. These young are born helpless and need constant nurture and protection by their parents if any are to survive. With this biological bonding between parents and their offspring new behaviours emerged such as care for the young and support for the weak.

The best things in life have fleas.

As mammals evolved, this instinctual bonding also evolved. It became love. Generosity, compassion, empathy, loyalty, altruistic cooperation, a willingness to die to protect others, these are forms of love shown, not only by humans, but by all great mammals.

Dolphins support injured animals by swimming under them and pushing them to the surface so they can breathe. They've also saved the lives of land-animals, including humans, who have fallen into the water, by carrying them to the safety of land. Orang-utans and chimpanzees are not even closely related yet orang-utans will feed hungry chimpanzees. They have also been observed taking care of the young of other species who have been orphaned. Elephants help each other in distress, grieve for their dead and feel a range of emotions just like us. Humpback whales often save other species in ways that offer little benefit to them. Scientists have said they cannot explain these behaviours other than describing them as acts of 'kindness'.

Love was born in the warm hearts of mammals. This love then evolved from a simple instinctual bonding into a complex love that demonstrates compassion, empathy and selflessness, even rendering an individual willing to die so that those they love can live. This embodied mammalian love is the most real of all loves.

Abstract, 'spiritual' loves for a transcendental deity or disembodied ideal are not real unless they manifest in the body through our actions. The body is the source, the expression and the manifestation of all love. It is the body that suffers and therefore needs love. It is the body that experiences and feels love.

Once again religion has taken what belongs to the animal body and projected it skyward, falsely claiming this imaginary god is the source of all love.

What religion is God?

If there is a God of love then this God is an energy field that has been created by animals who suffer, bleed and die. It is certainly not the pre-existing pre-ordained love of a deity that serenely floats above it all. Anyway a god smiling down from on high will be useless to us as we navigate the apocalyptic ecological destruction soon to overwhelm us. We need an embodied real living animal love in the body when we're struggling to grow food else starve, dying from antibiotic resistant diseases, suffering from the blind panic and violence around us when people realise what has been done to them. The challenges lie here on Earth, and here is where we must make the love we so desperately need to save us from ourselves.

Embodied love is alive, feeling, and spontaneous. It makes being alive good. We may have projected this goodness onto mythical figures in the heavens, angels, saints, heavenly beings of light and the main man, God, but this goodness resides in the living animal-body. And we need it here and now, not after we're dead.

I aim to die young as late as possible.

To navigate the current Mass Extinction something other than mere survival has to give meaning to our lives and deaths. The vast deaths of the mass extinction are utterly heartbreaking, yet when we understand our deaths will give birth to new life forms, life can become more conscious and loving. When we realise our lives will enrich life for future generations, there is some solace for our grief that all is not completely lost. When we sense that how we have lived creates realities that vibrate in the energy fields of existence outside space and time forever, even death is experienced as part of life. And when we come fully conscious of our experience of being alive we know that the energy of life is what matters more than anything else.

32 Love's Body

> *Outside the dimensions of space and time lies a mystery beyond our comprehension. One part of that mystery is that life renews itself through death and so whether we live or die is not the deeper meaning of it all. What we create while alive is far more important than mere survival.*

When we die we give ourselves back to life. Freedom, laughter, beauty, wisdom, music, healing, authenticity, play, whatever has been our particular love, this becomes our creative offering back to existence as we leave. And in this gift of ourselves we live on in life forever.

If love is the gift of oneself then death from this perspective is an act of love. We are giving ourselves, and all we have created while alive, back to life. Love therefore renders our lives greater than our deaths. Our legacy is whatever we have had the courage to love.

God wants you to give him your soul.   Yeah well, Satan's up for buying it.

We could say, the dead do not leave their legacy behind them - they become it. Some aspects live on in the turbulence of our unresolved issues in the lives of those who knew us. Other aspects live on as a legacy of the spirit that is eternal. Some aspects are food for future life forms. But, whatever the form of our eternity, our legacy is created through how we live life while in the body.

The love that is the gift of oneself transcends death. This is the triumph of love over death - not that one survives, but that what one has created lives on.

If you love me, give me your heart.   But then you'll have two and I'll have none.

Each species of animal and plant makes a unique contribution to the energy fields of existence. Perhaps elephants create a vast remembering, dolphins, a cosmic energy field of play, beetles, a unique and indefinable beetle-ness, trees, a deep rooted witnessing. Who knows? We don't; we're human. Our responsibility lies in the creation of the *human* gift to the cosmos - a love of life all the more conscious because of our alienation from life.

From this perspective, the deaths of the 6th Mass Extinction will release mammalian love, alongside all the other energies created by life on Earth, into the energy fields of existence. There it becomes part of the creative force of the universe. The energies of life, released on death into the energy fields beyond the dimensions of space and time, may even be what called existence into being in the first place. What else did? God? Prana? The Big Bang? Pangu? The Word?

Perhaps the creatures created the Creator who created them. Perhaps these words are merely fingers pointing to the same truth – that the source of it all is an energy field of love that evolved through the trillions of lives and deaths of Earth's creatures, over millions of years. The Mystery, by definition, cannot be defined.

Reality is just a guess in the dark.

Alongside the heart-breaking loss of life, it might be that the mass mammalian deaths of the Anthropocene Extinction will liberate a vast energy-field of love. Perhaps this love bequeaths to the cosmos the very realities that existence needs to fulfil itself. Perhaps this is, in part, what the whole weird and wonderful adventure has all been about - the creation and release of a love of life that transcends mere survival in order that existence can give birth to itself - and then wonderfully, gloriously and utterly magnificently come to life.

In which case through our love and the release of that love back to life when we die, we are playing our part in the creation of existence and the evolution of life. And despite everything, this vast drama was always meant to unfold exactly as it is.

Everything happens for a reason.

Yeah – sometimes the reason is that you're stupid.

How the eco-apocalypse is unfolding, what exactly is occurring and why it is happening are ultimately questions about events beyond our comprehension. The sixth mass extinction is another cycle of a vast cosmic mystery. Our job is to live in ways that manifest wisdom, beauty, freedom, integrity, and a consciousness and love of all life. And we must do this here and now, while we are still alive and in a body. So let's get on with it.

Whatever our nationality, race or gender, whether we live in a hut or a manor house, on a farm or in a city, whatsoever our age, status, class, colour, gender, education, wealth, or privilege, let us love life so totally we lose ourselves in that love. Whatever we love - sport, music, family, friends, music, cooking, the rainforest, knitting, children, dogs, whales, a garden, freedom, sailing, mountain climbing, laughter, mathematics, sex, freedom, truth, beauty, designing wallpaper, playing – let us give ourselves to it so completely we love this life enough to be willing to die for it.

That way we free ourselves from fear and find ourselves back in the paradise we were exiled from all those aeons ago. When, in order to become human, we divided life into good and evil and lost the living knowledge that *all* life is good, even death. On our return we will bring back with us the many gifts we created in our long journey away. And all life will celebrate our return.

The universe is a large place – perhaps the largest.

33   Love & Life in an Eco-Apocalypse.

We are facing an unfolding catastrophe of so many dimensions and aspects it is impossible to predict what will actually happen. We know only that it will be an apocalyptic destruction on a global scale never seen before. Not only will every level of human culture and society be destroyed, life itself will be devastated.

Today is the first day of the rest of this mess.

This catastrophic future is unprecedented. None of us knows how to navigate or deal with it. There is no wisdom of the elders, wise people who have seen it all before, to advise us, nor are there maps from history to guide us, and with such a vast complexity of interdependent factors and tipping points, scientific predictions cannot be relied upon either.

This is why one suggestion is to get together with friends, families, comrades, people in your community or neighbourhood, and begin to plan for the future with original and creative possibilities for how to live. Another is to sit and meditate on what the eco-crisis means for you and those you love. Another is to tune in on the instinctive wisdom of the body and let that guide you.

You might find yourself pondering how to grow food, build shelters and fix solar panels. You might think about how to keep healthy, cure disease, first aid, and learn herbal medicine. Maybe you will explore how to care for children, how to teach them vital skills, what they need for their social and emotional well-being, as well as their physical survival. Perhaps you will feel drawn to have meetings with others where you share feelings and fears about yourselves and the crisis, bringing hopes, conflicts, confusions and irrational dimensions of yourselves to the table. You might explore how to handle disliking certain people, feeling angry and hurt by each other, or being sexually attracted to someone not your partner. You might consider how the chaos of people living and working together can be ordered and how to protect yourselves and your community. Which will become a real issue when society's structures for dealing with violence and looting break down when starvation and mass migrations begin.

You should write a to-do list everyday.   I do, but nobody does it.

If community is the way you feel called, you have to trust the wisdom of the community or group that you belong to. The list of what you explore cannot be determined by anyone other than yourselves.

Though whatever your path, let there be a love of life right in the heart of all you do. At least then if the worst happens you can face death with a love for the life you have had. And of course the worst is going to happen, even if we don't know when.

Ultimately the challenge is not about survival, it is about how to live well and die well. This is because in the end, whether as individuals or as a species, the chances are we are not going to survive. Maybe a few pockets of human beings will stagger on in a some wilderness areas or what is left of the Amazonian jungle, but these will have such a depleted bio-diversity to support them they will struggle to survive and perhaps will be merely food for the rising stars of whatever is the dominant species in the next cycle of life.

It has been hard to face but after a lifetime full of visions and dreams for a better world, all my hopes have ended. I have had to painfully and slowly make my peace with the death and destruction of all I have loved.

It's time to go 'OM'.

Though it is not true that all I love will be destroyed. Life itself will not be destroyed.

Life will continue. After heartbreak, rage and despair, I now understand what is happening is inevitable. Also that it has a meaning beyond my own individual desires for survival.

My way to navigate through this has become to live each moment as fully engaged with life as I can. This includes the wonders and beauty of life *and* its tragedy and anguish. Then when death comes for me, I will die as I have lived – alive to the whole experience. Which means when I die, even if I am in pain and afraid, I will die with a love of life in my heart - and that is a deeper fulfilment than mere survival.

There is an African blessing: 'When death comes to find you, may he find you alive.' When death comes to you, I hope he finds you alive too.

What have you planned for the future?

Lunch.

I mean for the long-term future.

Dinner.

The path to wisdom is a journey that involves your heart breaking many times. A heart that remains unbroken is a fortress against the pains of life and death and nothing can come into it. When our hearts are broken wide open, all life can find a home in us. But only love can break your heart. Death is one of life's greatest teachers about what really matters - life and love.'
Chogyam Trungpa Rinpoche.

A broken heart is an open heart.

loveandextinction@gmail.com

Thank you to:

Maid of Kent Beetle, Giraffe Weevil, Giant Stag Beetle, Brush Jewel Beetle, Eulichas Serricornis, Fat Clown Beetle, Brassy Big-Eyed Beetle, Red Spotted Lily Weevil, Fiddler Beetle, Macrolycus Flabellatus, Merchant Grain Beetle, Ondontolabis Cuvera, Mosaic Round Sand Beetle, Proagoderus Rangifer, Phycosecis Limbata, Southern Rain Beetle, Polycesta Costata Costata, Rhipicera Femorata, Proculus Goryi, Leconte's Rain Click Beetle, Ox Beetle, Theodosia Viridiaturata, Pictured Rove Beetle, Roughened Darkling Beetle, Tricondyla Aptera, Semiotus Luteipennis, Asemobius Caelatus, Fulcida Monstrosa, Broscus Cephalotes, Sphaeridium Scarbaeoides, Delta Green Ground Beetle, Lycus Malanurus, Eurhinus Magnificus, Cow-Faced Anthribid, Dogbane Beetle, Macleay's Long-Armed Chafer, Cychrus Caraboides, Gymnetis Stellata, Amphizoa Insolens, Philabus Viridans, Heterosternus Buprestoides, Spider Weevil, Parorobitis Gibbus, Chilena Magnificent beetle, Golofa Porteri, Forekd Fungus Beetle, Agathidium Pulchrum, Byctiscus Rugosus, Thief Weevil, Julodimorpha Saundersii, Notolioon Gemmatus, Stenus Cribricollis, Dicaelus Purperatus, Necrophilus Subterraneus, Japanese Rhinoceros Beetle, Cupes Capitatus, Oxypius Peckorum, Mecynorhina Torquata, Esemephe Tumi,Cossyphus Hoffmannsegghii, Bearded Weevil, Saprinus Cyaneus, Red Rove Beetle, Eleodes Acutus, Necrophila Formosa, Helea Spinifer, Mecynorhina Savagei, Kibakoganea Sexmaculata, Hyperion Schroetteri, Convergent Lady beetle, Lenax Mirandus, Melobasis Regalis Regalis, Agreeable Caterpillar Hunter, Five-Horend Rhinoceros Beetle, Cherry Weevil, Polybothris Auriventris, Inca Clathrata Sommeri, Two-Spotted Weevil, Dialithus Magnificus, Borolinus Javanicus, American Crudely Carved Wrinkle Beetle, Damaster Blaptoides, Royal Goliath Beetle, Stephanorrhina Guttata, Elephastomus Proboscideus, Transvestie Rove Beetle, Kentucky Cave Beetle, Pale-Legged Gazelle Beetle, Splendid Earth-Boring Beetle and Calognathus Chevrolati Eberlanzi.

As my friend Barbara said, 'Who'd have thought beetles knew so much!'

Thank you too to everyone who played a part in the creation of this book.